LAX-Files

LAX-Files:
Behind the Scenes with the Los Angeles Cast and Crew

Erica Fraga

CreateSpace.com

LAX-Files

Copyright © 2010 by Erica Fraga

All rights reserved. No part of this book may be reproduced in any part by any means without the written permission of the author, except by a reviewer, who may use brief excerpts in a review.

The X-Files is a trademark of Twentieth Century Fox. *LAX-Files* was not approved, endorsed, authorized, or licensed by Twentieth Century Fox.

Cover design by Melanie Muller

Printed and bound through CreateSpace.com

ISBN: 1451503415

EAN-13: 9781451503418

Table of Contents

Dedication, by R.W. Goodwin..page 9

Forward, by Frank Spotnitz..page 13

Please Stay on the Highlighted Route....................................page 17

The X-Files..page 19

Fight the Future..page 21

Fight the Future Filming Locations..page 37

Season Six: A New Beginning..page 41

Season Six Filming Locations..page 53

Season Seven: A Turning Point...page 87

Season Seven Filming Locations...page 107

Season Eight: Changing of the Guard...................................page 167

Season Eight Filming Locations...page 179

Season Nine: Believe in the Future.......................................page 213

Season Nine Filming Locations...page 227

Don't Stop Believing...page 239

Acknowledgements..page 241

LAX-Files is dedicated to late director, Kim Manners.

You are missed Kim.

Dedication

I met Kim Manners in the spring of 1995 during the second season of *The X-Files*. At the time, the show was rapidly becoming an enormous international hit, and all of us were bending under the enormous strain of producing it. We had struggled to find directors who could handle the episodes. Unlike most series with regular characters in established sets and locations, each of *The X-Files* was a little, separate movie unto itself and many directors were overwhelmed by the challenge. Jim Wong and Glen Morgan, Co-Executive Producers at the time, along with our director of photography, John Bartley, who had all worked previously with Kim at Cannell Productions, persuaded me to hire Kim for an episode. At that point, Kim was a very successful episodic director, but there was no assurance he was going to be any more successful at handling *The X-Files* than a lot of the other episodic directors who had paid us visits.

Kim's first episode was *Die Hand Die Verletzt* in which he had to deal with satanic rituals, frogs raining down on Mulder and Scully, a character who has a psychotic breakdown, an enormous boa constrictor that devours another character, and on and on. Kim's work was masterful. He clearly had great reserves of talent that had never been fully exposed to the world. The uniqueness of *The X-Files* along with the consistent high quality of the scripts from Chris Carter and our amazing writers provided Kim with a canvas to show the world what a true artist he was. We immediately made him a producer on the show, so that we would have exclusive call on his services.

Along with his directing talent, we also acquired a co-worker who was a fun-loving, dedicated soul who enriched all of our lives. He was one of the most decent human beings I ever had the pleasure to know, and possessed a wonderfully wicked sense of humor. (I still have a framed autographed photo from Kim from his first colonoscopy that shows a part of him that very few people have ever seen.)

Losing Kim at such an early age was a true tragedy. Fortunately, he has left a body of work that will survive for generations, and those of us who were lucky enough to have Kim in our lives will have our memories of him forever.

- R.W. Goodwin

I would like to extend a very special thank you to Kathy Roe, Jessica Gunderson, Chelsea Gunderson, and Marlene Manners for your help and support on this book.

Forward

"Where do your ideas come from?" It's the question I'm asked most often, and the hardest one to answer. That's because writers don't order up ideas, like picking dishes on a menu. Rather, the ideas mysteriously – sometimes, almost miraculously – are delivered to them from their subconscious minds. It's only after the idea has been received that a writer can try deciphering its origin and meaning.

It's been nearly 20 years since *The X-Files* began -- not as a TV series, but as an idea. Chris Carter has tried to explain where it came from. He's acknowledged that he was influenced by a terrifying TV movie, *The Night Stalker,* he saw as a kid. And an equally terrifying 1991 movie, *The Silence of the Lambs.* But how did he arrive at this particular idea? Why two FBI agents – Mulder, the believer, Scully, the skeptic – investigating cases bearing the designation 'X' for unsolved?

Whatever magical imaginary calculus created it, *The X-Files* is an idea that has lived on, not just in Chris' mind, but in the minds of millions of fans around the world. But back in 1995, when Kim Manners first joined the series, it was still a relatively new idea. Two key writers from the series' first season, Glen Morgan and James Wong, were leaving. Kim had been brought in to direct their final episode, *Die Hand Die Verleltz*. (After "The Wongs" returned for part of the fourth season, it became the first of two brilliant farewell episodes they wrote.)

Like so much of the key talent at Ten Thirteen Productions – Glen and Jim, David Nutter, Rob Bowman, Bryan Spicer, John Kousakis, etc. -- Kim had spent years working for Stephen Cannell Productions in Vancouver. He was older than the rest of us, having started directing 20 years earlier on *Charlie's Angels*, but he had more passion and fire than even the youngest of us. Kim had drifted into a professional and creative backwater over the years, and he was eager for a chance to prove just how talented he was. He immediately seized *The X-Files* as that opportunity.

Most of the writers at *The X-Files* were calm and understated, not prone to displays of emotion or even raising our voices. But not Kim. Kim didn't like you – he *loved you, man*. He wasn't going to do a good job directing an episode -- he was going to *direct the shit out of it*. He didn't want anyone to go to work – he wanted us all to *kick it in the ass*. (It's hard to write about Kim without using a lot of italics. And expletives.)

Of course his enthusiasm was infectious. Just about everyone who worked with Kim – from the writers and producers to the cast and crew – loved him. You knew he was going to give his all on every episode, every day. It inspired you to give your all, too. To honor Kim the way his enthusiasm demanded. And Kim *loved* what he was doing. There was no place he'd rather be, even if it was freezing-ass cold in the GVRD at 4 a.m. on a Saturday. "I'm like a pig in shit," he'd say.

His work was as emotional as he was. Kim's camera was always moving, fluid – never neutral. He made sure he had something to say at every moment. Kim needed to understand a script inside out before he would direct it – he'd read it over and over again, making it his own. Then he'd map out his shots – his "homework," he called it. When he described the shots he envisaged in a scene, and how it would ultimately cut together, he delivered a performance to rival any actor's, with lots of heartfelt description and hand gestures.

Kim's love made Chris' magical idea burn brighter, deeper, stronger and more beautifully. His nearly three-season rivalry with fellow in-house director Rob Bowman resulted in a stunning visual evolution of the series and – it's not too much to say – television itself. When people talk about *The X-Files* being cinematic or a little movie every week, they're talking about the visual ambition and sophistication that Rob and Kim brought to the series during those seminal years, from Season 2 to 4. (It's nothing short of disgraceful that neither Rob nor Kim was ever nominated by the DGA or Television Academy for their work on *The X-Files*.)

Kim stayed with the series after *Fight the Future* was released, and production moved from Vancouver to Los Angeles. But his passion never dimmed. He was as eager, engaged and excited directing the final two hours of the series as he was directing his first episode. How could you not love a man like that?

Even now, it's hard to accept that Kim is gone. It doesn't seem possible that someone so full of life could ever pass away. But in a very real sense, he hasn't. Kim's brilliant mind and beautiful spirit live on in every frame of every episode he directed. You can see his passionate imagination in his work. And his work has become part of our imaginations now, too.

This book chronicles the years that *The X-Files* spent in Los Angeles. There would be no *X-Files* were it not for the contributions of so many talented people who worked on the series in Vancouver during its first five seasons. But – despite the conventional wisdom – the cast and crew in Los Angeles built upon that work, and reached new creative heights. Over the course of nine television seasons and two feature films, the idea that was born in Chris' mind grew into a beautiful, elaborate story that will continue to fascinate and entertain for years to come.

- Frank Spotnitz

Please Stay On the Highlighted Route

In October 2008, I travelled up to British Columbia to take my own X-Files location tour with the help of Todd Pittson's *X Marks the Spot*, along with two very dear Canadian friends. Upon returning, I did some asking around and found out there was no location book for the Southern California X-Files spots. Inspiration struck, and I contacted location manager Ilt Jones and began to assemble what would become the location aspect of *LAX-Files*.

When news of Kim Manners passing reached the fandom in January 2009, I decided to combine my idea for a location guide with a book about Kim and his time on *The X-Files*. After checking with Frank Spotnitz and Kim's family, in March 2009 to January 2010, I began to assemble personal photos, commentary tracks, and cast and crew interviews to honor Kim. Sadly, negotiations with FOX did not go as planned and all personal photos of the cast and crew had to be removed from publication. What remains of *LAX-Files* is a collection of cast and crew's memories of their time on *The X-Files*, specifically in Los Angeles and their memories of the great Kim Manners.

Finding and visiting iconic locations from the show, like the haunted mansion from *How the Ghosts Stole Christmas* and Rob's apartment from *Hungry,* was a memorable experience. Discovering that remarkable locations, such as the condominium from *Agua Mala* and the mobile home park from *Je Souhaite,* had been torn down was disappointing. That being said, there are some sites that are on private land and you do need to check with the facility for visiting hours or tour dates.

While *LAX-Files* is no longer about Kim Manners, it is dedicated to his memory. I hope you find as much pleasure in reading this book as I did in putting it all together.

100 percent of the books profits will be donated to the American Cancer Society in Kim's name, at the request of his family, so be sure and buy two or three copies.

- Erica Fraga

The X-Files

Fight the Future

When *The X-Files* aired back in 1994, there was nothing else like it on television. Most fans would argue there is nothing like it on television today. Working on a show with such high standards clearly brought some people into the spotlight. Nearly every person I spoke with had a great deal of appreciation for series creator, executive producer, writer, and director Chris Carter. "Chris was my mentor when I first began with the series," Rob Bowman tells me. "He was a gas, asking me to do all the cool things I wanted to do."

As Laurie Holden, who played Marita Covarrubias, fondly recalls, "Chris Carter was definitely my mentor when I began with the series. It all began with him. He created this character and cast me in the role. Everything that he wrote for my character was interesting and thought provoking. He always had a wonderful way of coming up with things that one would never expect and I loved, loved, loved my character. It was a privilege and pleasure to have played a role in the mythology; to have been a part of the show for so many years. Cassandra Spender was another great creation. In fact, *Patient X* is one of my favorite episodes by far. I loved everything about this episode, from the introduction of Veronica Cartwright's character, to the filmic genius of that mass of people at the bridge, gazing at the heavens waiting for another alien ship to arrive; with the faceless men setting everyone on fire, and that fiery final sequence - it was absolute brilliance across the board. I also loved it as an actress because it was challenging and fun. To play a scene in Russian was so incredibly surreal and fantastic. Studying the rhythms of the language and learning the dialect authentically from scratch was one of the coolest things I have been asked to do as an artist. I do remember during *Patient X* that Nic Lea and I came up with very creative ways to remember our Russian. After countless hours of huddling together with our dialect coach we'd come up with these fun ways to test ourselves to know if we had really nailed it. Show tunes come to mind, but I also remember this one time my dialect coach had me call a Russian friend of his on his cell phone to see if he could understand me. I passed the test."

"Chris has found a way to make science fiction – again, I always go back to this emotion, pathos, compassion," Kim Manners told *The Complete X-Files* author Matt Hurwitz in a 2002 interview. "You've got to feel for not only our heroes, but for our anti-heroes."

"I'm really quite proud of the episodes that we pulled off that were both funny, strange, and mysterious," David Duchovny tells me. "Some of them were written by Chris, The Wong's, and Darin Morgan – the classics."

"The most important advice I received came from Chris, Rob, and Kim," Bill Roe tells me. "All three of them helped me because they were the main people that came from Vancouver. Michael Watkins also helped me when he joined the director's list. Those guys really pushed me, all of us in fact, into really going a lot further than anyone else has ever gone. There was always a thought of 'don't be afraid of going dark', 'don't be afraid of taking a chance and making it dark'. Just don't be afraid of it. It's not easy, so you have to learn how to do it. It's not just turning lights off and on, which we did all the time, but it's also separation of layers; you have to create this darkness. There is a fine line between going dark and still being able to see everything."

"I definitely learned a lot working with Chris. I worked on the Pilot episode and we got a call saying they needed a vortex of leaves, and somebody was going to build this rig with fake leaves on a wire and spin them around," replies Mat Beck when asked who he considers a mentor on the show. "I said we're not going to do it that way, so I began to work on the Pilot and I remember riding up in a car with Chris and we were talking about the nature of the forests in Vancouver and the human psyche and how dark and mysterious it is."

I asked Producer Paul Rabwin who influenced him in his career. "Obviously in many respects Chris Carter did," Paul reports. "I had met him before the series and was really impressed with his style. I was one of the firsts who came on to the series. I had met Bob Goodwin, who was a combination of a mentor and a colleague. He is a very close friend, going back to 1971 or so. I have great respect for Bob, who introduced me to Chris and to Jim Wong, Glen Morgan, and Howard Gordon. These were the guys from the very beginning that were most influential for me because I kind of saw the shape the series was taking and I had never seen anything like that. It was ground breaking on so many levels. To be with the creative team so early on was really exciting. At that time, I had been in the business for twenty-three years, so I was not a newbie learning the ropes. Pretty much everyone was younger than me, so I was being mentored and influenced by a new generation and it was great for me to experience that. Kim Manners came on in the second season and Dave Nutter, who was pretty young at the time, opened my eyes to a lot of elements of directing. Probably the one I attached to early on was Rob Bowman since we had been friends in the past as well. He has an extremely visual sense and his vision was quite impressive. The Nutter-Bowman-Manners triangle of directing was unparalleled in the business. It was a great environment to be in, no question about it. I learned very quickly, that being older and experienced, if you were smart, you opened yourself up to gain many more experiences and learn from those that know more than you do. The fact that I had been working in the business for a while didn't mean that I knew much. I really got a great deal out of working on the show those early years."

In addition to the wonderful advice and guidance that both Kim and Chris provided to the cast and crew, others were ready to lend a hand. "The most helpful and encouraging person, the one who helped me think about lighting was Rob Bowman," says Bill Roe. "We would sit down and have these conversations about lighting; why we do this; why he does this. [The show] was in Vancouver for five years, so we'd discuss how we could make it better [in LA], and how could we use the locations that Vancouver didn't have there. We knew we could not re-create the Vancouver overcast, grey color. But at night we could wet it all down so we could still get that feeling. We talked about keeping the look and feel of the show, making it interesting with what we have, and not trying to make it what Vancouver is or was. Rob helped me understand what we were doing and why they wanted to do it that way. He taught me a lot about the look of the show, and to this day, I'm still working with Rob. *Castle* starts shooting Wednesday."

"I have to thank Michael Watkins for bringing me into the family," adds Harry Bring. "I had just come off of a seven year run on *Melrose Place* and Aaron Spelling had no new project where I could go to. When you're locked up on a show for so long, people forget your name. Michael heard that I was available, so he brought me in. He definitely cast a wonderful crew that set the environment for everyone to work in. Bernadette 'Bernie' Caulfield was so nurturing to me as well. Bernie also saw to my promotions, even as she exited the show, which allowed me to become a producer for the last two and a half years. We were all labored with taking over a show that has a certain expectation; a certain way of operating in an environment for five years. It was shocking to the industry down here in Los Angeles since it was definitely not normal."

The "Vancouver Ethic" was something that was not limited to the work going on behind the camera. As Chris Carter shares, "Something that I'll never forget is the night we burned down the barn in *Post Modern Prometheus*. I don't know how we accomplished it. We put a bunch of extras in a barn carrying lit torches and there is hay everywhere. One misstep, one false move and that barn really would have gone up in flames. Not only did we have extras running out of the barn, but we had animals, including horses, and a horse actually ran over one of the extras. It was a big scene so I did not see that happen, but I heard about it and I ran over to the extra, who was muddy and filthy dirty, and I asked him if he was okay. He tells me, 'Yeah. Did you get the shot?' That is perfectly indicative of the kind of work ethic you got in Vancouver."

As it is with most shows, many people work very hard behind the scenes to make sure the ship runs smoothly. Creator and executive producer, Chris Carter, took time out of his busy schedule to try and thank as many people as he could for the show's success.

"There are many parents to the baby that is *The X-Files*: Randy Stone, Peter Roth, Charlie Goldstein, Bob Goodwin, Dan Sackheim, Bob Mendel, Glen Morgan and James Wong, Howard Gordon, Paul Rabwin," shares Chris. "It would be unfair to leave people out and say that this is the entire list, but I would say anyone who worked on the Pilot and the first season of the series was my angels in a way. They deserve to be honored because they contributed so much."

The release of *The X-Files: Fight the Future,* was one of the most anticipated movies of 1998. With five seasons under its belt, *X-Files* fans all over the world were waiting for answers. What changes would be in store for the characters? Would the X-Files be returned to Mulder and Scully? Would the government finally acknowledge the existence of extraterrestrials?

The show's migration to Los Angeles from Vancouver, British Columbia, where it had filmed for five years, brought many changes. Aside from the obvious location change, new crew members were brought on. Rob Bowman, who had been a director since 1994 on the show, has this to say about this change.

"There were a whole bunch of things that were harder on the movie [locations] because I didn't have my crew from Vancouver," says Rob. "The short hand was not there, so it was a lot more literal direction as opposed to people just knowing where I'm going to go with the way I make decisions, as I did in Vancouver. I'm back at square one with all these movie people who are moving from big movie to big movie, and don't have the emotional investment that the Vancouver crew has; it's just another big job for them. So to convey the passion, the investment of time that we had put in to get to the place where we had the privilege of making the movie, was a daily challenge; an annoying challenge because there was nothing I could do about it. No disrespect to the [LA] people who made it since they were very professional and highly experienced, but they weren't there for the four or five years it took to get there. There was the scene with the boy falling into the hole and the fire trucks and circus trucks showing up. I wanted to shoot that backlit by the sun. Somebody had put the lunch tent right in the shot. I showed up to shoot that day and had my plans all lain out. When I looked where I was going to master from, just off camera left, in line with the row of houses was the big lunch tent. I could not shoot that with the same cinematic vocabulary as I had shot the series on and how I would shoot the exterior. It was very aggravating to me since it was a big day and a big deal. I had to make camera placement adjustments outside of my comfort zone so that I wouldn't see a lunch tent. I was frustrated by that, and I know my Vancouver crew would have never done that."

"I enjoyed the crews that I worked with on *The X-Files*, both Vancouver and Los Angeles," remembers Mitch Pileggi. "They were a family and I cherish my time and friendships with them. It's great, because when I go up to Vancouver, like for *Supernatural*, I have a chance to work with the same guys as I did on *The X-Files*. It's such a treat to work with them again. When we moved down to Los Angeles from Vancouver, they sent the furniture from Skinner's office down. The first day at the FOX studios, I was messing with Skinner's desk and I open up the main drawer and some of the Vancouver crewmembers had taped a note for me. It was so touching; they said some wonderful and beautiful things to me. Here it was, first day back, and I almost started crying just looking at that note. It was hard to say good-bye to people like that, and then to say good-by again to the Los Angeles crew when the show wrapped was hard as well. I had two families that I was leaving."

"We were in Canada the first five seasons," Kim told author Matt Hurwitz. "And then David Duchovny decided he couldn't take it anymore; it was too wet. After I was done kissing David, we moved to Los Angeles, and I was the happiest guy on the freeway. I was the only idiot smiling in the morning. I love Vancouver and I loved working up there; we had a great crew. But I started in Vancouver in 1986; I directed, well really Fox's first one-hour pilot, *21 Jump Street*, with Johnny Depp, and Peter Deluise, and Steven Williams, etc. And because we sold that and I directed 20 or 25 of those and suddenly I was an American director who was doing a lot of television up there. And I found myself working up there a lot. I went to Australia in '88 during the writers' strike and did the remake of *Mission Impossible*. And then in '94 I did *Brisco County*, but every other year since '86, I was up in Vancouver. So I was just as tired of the weather as David was, because after a while, and after you're not in your 30's anymore; you realize that rain should be appreciated through a window. It's not all that fun to stand in 15, 16 hours a day. And that's what we were shooting. We don't shoot those hours here in Los Angeles. But because the labor costs up there are so cheap, we'd shoot 15, 16 hours a day. And it takes its toll. So it was – again, there's been a lot of refreshing changes along this road that has been *The X-Files*. Moving it from Vancouver to [Los Angeles] was refreshing."

The location of filming wasn't the only thing that changed. Composer Mark Snow had to adapt his now famous theme for the big screen. "Knowing that this was a movie score and not a television score, I was thinking bigger and outside the box of synth music," continues Mark. "The style of music was not difficult, but in my mind I was trying to imagine the synth mock ups that I had for them all to come and listen to. Dan Sackheim, Chris Carter, Rob Bowman, and Frank Spotnitz heard that and they said it was great. When the orchestra came around there were really no surprises getting it all orchestrated, and copied, and recording it. It was not something I was used to on a weekly basis, but it was something I definitely felt confident about. It was a little more challenging than the weekly shows."

Throughout the history of the series, many lucky fans have had the opportunity to be a part of the production of the show. "My friend

Olga was in Casey's bar when they were filming *Fight the Future,*" says fan Kathleen Keegan. "This was the first time she had ever met David Duchovny. She's Russian, and at the time had a really thick accent, which has decreased over the years. David was very sweet to her; asking all these questions about her background since he's part Russian."

"Prior to 9/11, a person could find a daily Shoot Sheet put out by the organization that grants location permits in the greater Los Angeles area. The sheets included location address along with hours of planned operation," shares fan Guy Jackson. "Since we knew *Blackwood* was the code name for *Fight the Future*, we could scan the Shoot Sheet for location shoots and basically just show up and watch."

"I had a day off from work and decided to check out the shoot located at the Mira Monte Apartments in Los Angeles," continues Guy. "I had no idea what scene(s) were to be shot, but the hours of operation were from late afternoon until early morning the next day. As I got closer to the location, I saw the cardboard sign with 'BW' and an arrow indicating where the circus was located."

Crew sign for Blackwood.
Photo courtesy of Guy Jackson

"Parking about a block from the street that was being used for the shoot, I happened to walk by the Star Wagons that had been placed there and past a security guard who was sleeping on the job," adds Guy. "Orange traffic cones and some LAPD prevented folks from walking up the street where the 'Farber's Apartment' shoot was going by, but that was ok. Parked along the cross-street, where I staked a spot, were various taxis that had Virginia license plates and Arlington locations on the doors so I thought I was in the right spot. After camping out for about an hour or so by myself, David Duchovny, with the infamous red script in his hand, and Martin Landau walked down the street from the shoot and past me on the cross-street to the Star Wagons I had passed earlier. As the sun was going down - the crew turned on lights they had strung in trees/bushes/etc."

"Not long after sunset, who should appear out of a nearby parking structure, but Chris Carter," exclaims Guy. "He was munching on a plate full of food so I figured the circus and craft services were located there. He saw me, recognized me and came over to chat for a bit. He was paranoid that I would see something and post spoilers online. People had already posted photos and information about the inflatable beehives out in the desert near Bakersfield, along with the artificial cornfields and helicopter action. I gave him a book, Art Linson's *A Pound of Flesh: Perilous Tales of How to Produce Movies in Hollywood;* I thought he would like. Chris said, 'Now, you're not going to post about what you saw tonight, will you?' I replied, 'What have I seen? A few cars with DC and Arlington addresses on them? David and Martin Landau?' He shook his head, but nevertheless said, 'Mum's the word, OK?' I agreed. He then headed up the street to the apartment. During this time, another fan stepped up to me from out of the shadows and asked if that was Chris Carter. I told her yes and that we knew each other from other events. From then on, Miss X stuck around so we kept each other company at the lonely, dark end of the street."

"Somewhere around 10:00pm we saw a person running down the street toward us," recalls Guy. "It was Chris Carter and he was yelling for me! Once he got to us, he asked me, 'Guy. Trivia question: where does Mulder live?' 'Uhhhhh,' I said, 'In an apartment?' He said, 'No. What is his address?' To which I replied, 'I don't know. I don't memorize such detailed trivia. I have a life!' He looked at me and slowly walked away back to the apartment. As he left, I asked him, 'Did I fail the trivia question?' Chris replied, 'Yeah,' and continued on. I felt horrible, but Miss X cheered me up by pointing out that he was the creator of the show and he didn't know the answer! We found out later that the exact address was not in the script and they needed that information so that Mulder could give the cabbie his address. Ever the sticklers for authenticity! After that excitement, Miss X and I stuck around until about 11 PM and decided to call it a day as there really wasn't any action occurring on our dark, lonely end of the street. Little did I know that this was setting me up for my next location shoot visit."

"I was at another exterior shot wherein Scully was placed in the bio-containment stretcher, put in the ambulance and when Mulder tried to stop the ambulance driver, he was shot," continues Guy. "Gillian had already done her scene before I got there so they were setting up for David getting shot. The fans were allowed to within about 10 feet of the action this time. I ran into Miss X from the Farber's Apartment location shoot and we both agreed to NOT use our cameras that night; just be respectful observers. She then told me that someone on the crew was asking about me. She didn't recognize the man and, after pointing him out to me, I didn't recognize him either. After introducing myself to him, I found out he was unit publicist Alex Worman. Chris Carter had given him the heads-up that I might show up for the shoot. Miss X and I stuck around for a few hours as they set up and actually performed the shot with David Duchovny being shot by the paramedic ambulance driver and the ambulance driving off up the street."

"The next part of the story is what fans love to hear," Guys states. "I decided to pull a joke. Rumor had it that *The X-Files* production staff was scouring various message forums, looking for, and squelching any spoiler information. I logged into the official Fox *X-Files* forum board and posted a message with the following (approximate) title: *Exclusive! Behind-the-scenes Spoiler Information on the "Blackwood" movie!* The body of the post consisted of several blank pages, so people had to scroll to the bottom to find out what was going on, and then a simple sentence of: *Ha ha, Chris! Just wanted to see how paranoid you really are!* Several visitors/fans to the forum board left replies to this message wondering what was going on, but I never told. A few days after that posting, I received a private message from Alex Worman. The message read: *Ha ha, Guy! Good joke. Nice meeting you the other night. Mission accomplished.*"

In addition to forgotten trivia, there were other technical issues that needed to be solved by the crew in order to make the film a success. "There was one particular moment shooting on the [Pemberton] glacier when David's Snow Cat fails and he has to hike," says Rob Bowman. "He doesn't know where he is or how close he is [to Scully]. Back then we weren't thinking of removing footprints digitally, we were just mapping it out. Well, we couldn't figure out how to get the Snow Cat in a vista shot to drive straight towards us and just have one set of footprints coming from the Snow Cat up to the buff where we shot David's ascension. There was no time to sit down and draw a map since the sun was going down so all I could think of was to let the Snow Cat driver take the long way around the edge of the bowl and then we'll tell him when to turn right and head straight towards us. The driver did just that and stopped on cue via radio. And then I told David to get out of the Snow Cat and walk right towards us, and he makes the only set of footprints in the snow. We put David below the summit and then the shot starts with the Snow Cat a distance. You don't see Mulder; you don't know where he is until he pops up into the foreground. It seems like a very simple moment, but I can tell you there were a lot of people on the verge of panic because David and I were leaving the next day so we had to get the shot right or we don't have the moment."

"You have to get on the helicopter by a certain time every day to get off the [Pemberton] mountain, or you're staying overnight," warns Rob Bowman. "When they first started building the ice station for the movie they told the construction department that they had to get those igloos built very quickly because if they did get stuck, the igloos would provide good, safe shelter in case a grizzly bear or wolverines showed up. There were a couple of things you didn't want to encounter up there. In fact, those guys did get fogged in one day, where the helicopter could not land or take off, and they spent the night in the igloos. The art department was bundled up, hoping the grizzlies weren't going to show up."

The crew and cast did have some time to relax as *Fight the Future* was being made, sometimes with shenanigans ensuing. "I remember spending one Saturday afternoon at the Vancouver airport with Kim and his old friend Cliff Bole," recalls series writer and director Vince Gilligan. "Kim had arranged to visit a 767 simulator owned by Canadian Airlines, the wonderful, now defunct airline that we used to fly from Los Angeles. This was one of those massive, zillion dollar simulators that sits two stories tall on big hydraulic lifts, and it was a real treat to try it out. Unfortunately, when my turn came to 'land' the 767, I crashed it too hard that the whole simulator lurched downward with a BANG! Kim and Cliff, who happened to be standing in the back talking, were caught off guard, and it threw them for a loop. They were both really annoyed at me, but I secretly thought it was hilarious. On the way back to the Sutton Place Hotel, they regaled me with the funniest, most profane stories of the famous television personalities they had worked with over the years. I'd love to be able to repeat them here, but I would get myself in trouble. At any rate, it was an absolute pleasure to learn from those guys and spend time hanging out with them. I will always be glad they thought to bring me along that day."

Fight the Future Locations

Federal Building
LA Center Studios
1202 W. 5th St.
Los Angeles, Ca
*** Also used to play as the Federal Statistics Center in 8x18 *Three Words*

This site is not hard to miss at all. It's is visible from the freeway and very easy to recognize as the federal building.

The federal building from *Fight the Future*. Photo by Erica Fraga

Casey's Bar
613 S. Grand Ave.
Los Angeles, Ca
***Also used in 9x01 *This Is Not Happening I*

Mulder's Apartment
1724 Edgemont Ave.
Los Angeles, Ca

Alvin Kurtzweil Apartment
751 S. Normandie Ave.
Los Angeles, Ca

Minor changes have been made to the building, but if you watch *Fight the Future* closely, you can clearly identify this building.

Alvin Kurtweil's Apartment building. Photo by Erica Fraga

Consortium Meeting Place
Athenaeum
551 S. Hill Ave.
Pasadena, Ca

Mulder's Hospital
St. Mary's Medical Center
1050 Linden Ave.
Long Beach, Ca

Season Six:
A New Beginning

The sixth season of *The X-Files* truly was a new beginning for the series. Moving the show to new locations, like the desert areas of Lancaster and Palmdale, gave the show a new look. The velvet green canopies of the lush Vancouver forest were replaced with arid, dry conditions seemingly in the middle of nowhere. The change was so memorable that one Season 6 crewmember had no difficulty recalling one particular night spent in the desert. "The crew was shooting in Palmdale or Lancaster for *Dreamland* and the entire crew witnessed a UFO streaming across the sky about 100 feet above the ground, 50 feet from the crew, travelling horizontally, and then disappeared. They never found out if it was real or just the Special Effects Department just proving how good they really are."

I asked Mark Snow how he felt the how had changed, if at all, when it moved from Vancouver to Los Angeles. "The best answer I can give for that is, as the show evolved from the pilot to the very last episode, whether I was conscious of it or not, I felt that I was constantly evolving with it. I tried to keep it real, fresh, and interesting. The mythology sort of had a set kind of sound and pallet. It was like doing a serial, episodic show where the sound had to be consistent throughout the storyline. It was the stand-a-lones that were a little more fun because it was really coming up with something new with each one of those individual episodes."

The X-Files score is easily recognizable even eight years after the show has ended. Mark had this to say about the creation of that unique theme as well as his approach to the film's score. "The story of *The X-Files* creation is as follows," begins Mark. "Chris sent over a whole bunch of CD's and he said I like the singing here; I like the guitar here; I like the drums here; I like the vocals here, a snip-it of this, and a fragment of that. I wrote four themes, one after the other, and they were all pretty good but he wanted something different. Chris kept saying he doesn't want it to be slick, produced, or an overly orchestrated thing. He wanted bare bones, simple and to the point. He was remarkably respectful, and after the fourth one, I said let's start from scratch and see what I can do. He walks out and my elbow went down on the keyboard and I had this digital echo machine on a certain rhythm, so when I played that piano accompaniment, which is 'Daba da dum;' it repeated itself, so it went 'daba du daba du daba du daba,' and I thought that was pretty good. Under that, I put this slow pad of combined synth things and a couple of percussion hits. I had this melody and I came up with these great six notes, but now it became a challenge to see what instrument was going to play it. I tried everything and finally stumbled upon this whistle sound from one of my samplers and I thought it was pretty good, but not loud enough or big sounding. Then my wife came in and said it was great. I called Chris back to check it out and the rest is history."

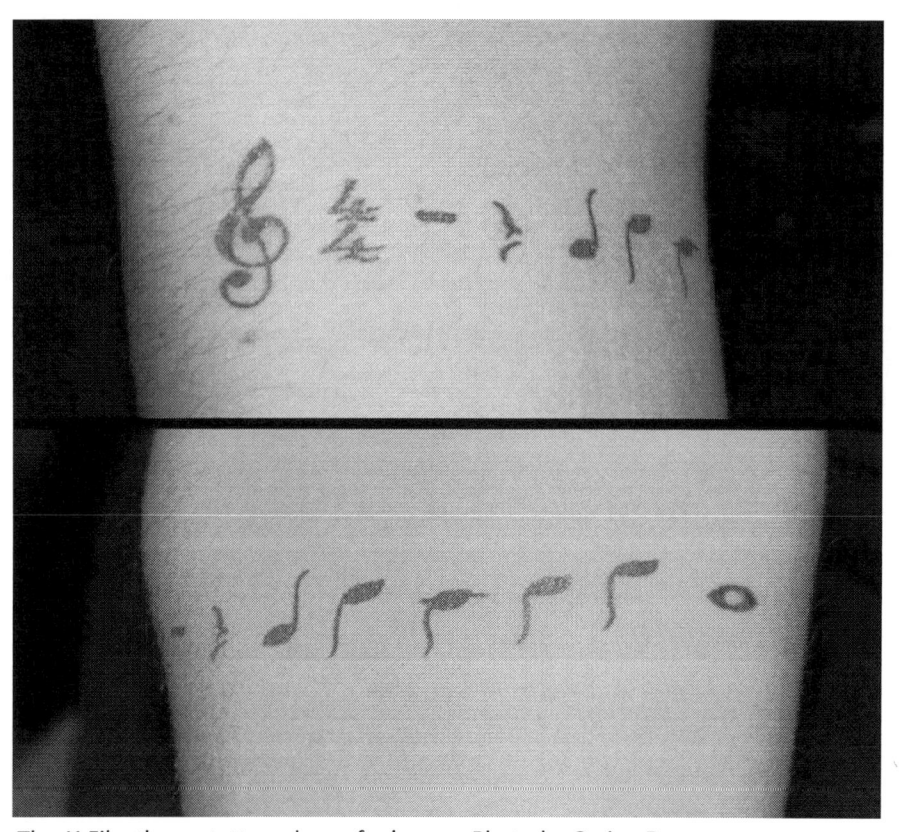

The X-Files theme tattooed on a fan's arm. Photo by Carina Brown.

Mark is also famously known for his creative and one of a kind sounds in both television and film. To capture the poignant moments in an episode, Mark would use many unique techniques. "I had the sound of a basketball bouncing on a gym floor from a few years before I started with *The X-Files*," states Mark. "By that time, it was overused, but I liked the sound and I wanted something like it. For *Arcadia*, for example, I found another kind of percussive sound that was similar. With my samplers and equipment I could tape these sounds and change them; pitch them up or down or reverse them. That was also part of the fun of *The X-Files* because you could have the sounds of real instruments mixed in with all kinds of sound designs and atmospheric sounds. Sometimes I thought the audience would say, 'that's not the score,' but many times it was a good combination of music and sound from my part. I remember the sound guys would be pissed in dubbing because Chris would tell them to make the music louder and get the sound effects lower. That was great for me, and it doesn't happen too often."

"I let the episode drive the music," reveals Mark. "It's the inspiration for me. I've often wondered about writing music without seeing a picture and it's a whole other discipline. With *The X-Files*, the mythology and the stand-alone episodes, whichever one it was, it was like doing a mini movie every week. I was also excited, no matter how tired I was or stressed out. It was always inspiring and great fun."

Not all aspects of the production could be categorized as inspiring and fun. "Memorizing the gobbledygook was something I struggled with on *The X-Files*," shares Bruce Harwood. "On *Blood*, my second appearance on the show I could not, for the life of me, get through the sentence about flies or whatever it was without screwing up. It took a bunch of takes to get it right, and then I screwed up the next line. After a couple years of practice, memorizing the gobbledygook was easy. When we moved onto *The Lone Gunmen*, the gobbledygook scenes were the easiest to do."

One of the main directors for the series, Rob Bowman was asked if he had a preference for directing the mythology or stand-a-lone episodes, and if he preferred to direct on location or on set. "I preferred to direct mythology based episodes since I always had a tough time with the monsters, since they always look so bad," replies Rob. "I had a tough time getting past how silly they looked, until you turned the lights off, put the scope on, and did all the things we do to make them look scary. No matter how terrific and key the prosthetics and make-up department was, it's just a guy in a rubber suit. And it just looked funny. I said if they wanted me to do a monster episode, it will have to be really dark so I can believe; with the right music and sound effects, I might get scared. I always told Chris, I'm happy to do a monster, but if it's at all possible I prefer to do a mythology episode. I was fascinated with the mistrust, the conspiracy, the mythology, and the betrayal stuff."

"The easiest place to shoot was anytime in Mulder's office because people are somewhat retracing their steps; you come in this door and go out that door," continues Rob. "You're really looking for variations on a theme, so you're not using the exact same camera placements every time. It's kind of home base and the audience likes to be there, so you don't want to make it too weird and too different so they don't recognize it."

Mulder's office. Photo courtesy of Adrienne Doucette.

In order for *The X-Files* to be as successful as it was, sacrifices had to be made; sleep was lost; lines were memorized, and shots were planned out to the most minuscule of details in order for favorite episodes to be made.

"I remember a lot of Saturday mornings where I drive home from work at 7am and pick up my newspaper as I was coming home, as all my neighbors were picking up their newspapers after waking up," remembers producer Harry Bring. "That's kind of the way it was for four years. We would have one unit with a 9 o'clock call and go until 11pm, and then we would have another unit start at 5pm and go until 6am or 7am. What I would do is prep all day with the next director and then sign off with both companies; one that had just started and one that was nearing the end of the day. I would go home about 8pm or 9pm and then set the alarm for 3am and go close the company that was finishing at 5 or 6 in the morning, and a third of the time that was Rob or Kim. This way I would know what they accomplished; what they didn't get; what they need. Since they worked nights, I would arrange for what they needed during the day. A lot of times, both units would be on nights; by Friday especially. I think this is one of the reasons why Kim and I hit it off originally, because the show was our life. I would say good night to my wife on Sunday night and say 'See you Saturday.' Unless you are on a sitcom, this is how it is in the industry."

Despite the long hours on location or set, the cast and crew found ways to entertain themselves with silly or crazy antics. "One of the craziest things I did on the show was to serenade Gillian to get her to come out of her trailer for a shoot," laughs Dan Sackheim. "She came out on the first attempt to stop me from singing."

Dean Haglund adds, "I borrowed our sound guy Mike's Dodge Viper and drove it around Vancouver a bit. I think that by the time I was in 6th gear I was exceeding the speed limit. Sorry Mike, if you are reading this."

"The craziest thing I ever saw on set was probably seeing Gillian's little girl, Piper, at home and happy as a clam and completely nonplussed by the strange creatures and aliens walking around the set and coming in and out of the trailer," remembers Laurie Holden. "Most kids that age would have been scared out of their minds by some of the special effects makeup and gore. Not this little kid; she was relaxed and in her element. I was very impressed by her cool. What an amazing child."

David Duchovny also shared his relaxation techniques in between takes. "I remember working on a show last year and someone said, 'David is happy in a scene if there is a ball in it.' And that is probably pretty true; it gives me something to do. To relax and get ready for a scene, I did a lot of yoga in my trailer. It allowed me to stay in shape and stay limber enough to be an action hero. Gillian is not an athlete, so it wasn't like I could play one on one with her. There was a hoop outside of our stages in Vancouver and one time Pete Chilcutt of the Vancouver Grizzlies came and shot with me one day so that was fun."

Never let it be said that *The X-Files* is not a learning environment for the young. Jeff Gulka, who played Gibson Praise, shared with me some warm memories on practically growing up on the series. "I really liked hanging out with David [Duchovny] because when I first started with the show I was really into Yo-Yo and he was really good too," remembers Jeff. "I challenged him to a Yo-Yo off, but he had better skills than me. He did show me some moves though. David was really good and talkative with me; we would have long conversations, and made me feel real comfortable. He even signed a Vancouver Grizzlies basketball for me, which I still have in my room on top of my dresser. He was a really great guy to work with. And Mitch [Pileggi] was really great. Gillian treated me just like everyone else and not like a little kid," continues Jeff. "I was present for some adult oriented jokes she told, most of which I didn't understand at the time, which helped make me feel like I was on everybody else's level and part of the team."

An exciting show like *The X-Files* had celebrity fans of the show clamoring for a guest appearance. Director Rob Bowman shared with me some of his favorite guest stars on the episodes he directed. "I was a fan of Bruce Campbell before I began to work with him, more so when I did work with him, and I will forever be a huge fan of Bruce," Rob conveys about his work on *Terms of Endearment*. "He had a tough role to play since the story was rough with burying babies and what not. He's a lot of fun to be around, but for him, the quality work comes first. Bruce wanted his rehearsals and requiring all the things that a top gun professional actor would require. It's one of the things I like so much about him. Whatever the part is, he wants to be the very best he can be. With David and Gillian, you can point your finger down a path and they just go that way; you don't have to walk with them since they know where they're going. With Bruce, he wants to keep up with David and Gillian, and he wanted to make sure he had the best environment to do that in. It was refreshing for me. This episode was a great homecoming for Bruce and me after directing him on *Brisco County, Jr.* After the cameras stopped however, David and Bruce were never ending with the jokes, giving each other a hard time, or quipping each other; oh my goodness. I can't remember anything specific, but everyday was so funny."

In addition to guest stars, Rob was able to see old friends from his past while working on *Arcadia*. "When I saw Abe [Benrubi] again, we gave each other great big bear hugs and it was great to see him after all these years. He had such a wisdom and maturity about him since I directed him on *Parker Lewis Can't Lose*. Anytime you have someone from your past come back around and they are doing well, you are happy for them. It's just like with Jack Black. I shot a second unit sequence in Kim's episode, *D.P.O.*, and then I had Jack in my very first movie called *Airborne*. We came full circle; it was a lot of fun seeing Jack again as well."

Not every celebrity fan wanted a guest spot, however. "I think one of the stupidest things I ever did on *The X-Files* was give my prop watch to Billy Corgan, of the Smashing Pumpkins when they were visiting the set," David says. "He gave me a hat, so I gave him Mulder's watch. I thought it was just a cheap prop watch. Turns out it was an expensive watch, according to Producer J.P. Finn."

The grueling production schedule didn't always allow for perfection. As it is with most projects, sometimes there is just not enough time to do it the way you want to, or, if given more time, would have done something differently. As Michael Watkins shares, "I would do this episode over and I wouldn't produce myself as a director," director Michael Watkins shares with me when I asked about episode, *Tithonus*. "I would put on my Chris Carter coat and just say, 'This is what I'm doing'. And I would have done it. I held myself responsible to finishing timely and there could have been more to the show. I thought Vince wrote a perfect script, but I would go back and do this over in a heartbeat. I would do it at a level, and a pace, and a rhythm that I want."

"I would have done *Millennium* differently, although I'm not sure how," continues Frank Spotnitz. "It was an episode we desperately wanted to make, in order to revisit Frank Black, but we had a terrible time figuring out how to merge the worlds of *Millennium* and *The X-Files*."

"I have a whole notebook of X-Files scribblings somewhere, but there was a *Lone Gunmen* idea I really wanted to do about the guys meeting their female counterparts," recalls writer Tom Schnauz. "I just had this image of seeing their distinct figures coming out from somewhere in silhouette, but when you see them, its' three conspiracy-minded women. Seeing who would be attracted to who would have been a blast."

"I had hoped that there would be one episode were we would have to help Pam Anderson flee from some MIB's and she would be grateful, but we would know that it would never work between us, and would set her free like a dove," continues Dean Haglund. "Or something like that."

And of course, when the show wrapped at the end of each filming season, a good time was had by all, usually at a local establishment, followed by some well deserved rest.

Season Six Filming Locations

6x01 The Beginning

Written By: Chris Carter
Directed By: Kim Manners
Summary: Proof of extraterrestrials may be found if Mulder and Scully can find the deadly creature hidden in the Arizona desert.

Shooting on location had both its perks and disadvantages to the show. While it allowed for a more realistic look, it can be difficult to secure the right location within a budget. Working on location, sometimes in the middle of nowhere, had its challenges but the crew always managed to pull it off.

"We shot up in Lancaster for *The Beginning*," states Producer Harry Bring. "Scouting that was all day event. Our shows were so big and both first and second unit so we went scouting in a van, or maybe two vans. After your prep, you show everyone else the locations you found and what direction you are shooting, what neighbors you are going to impact, and where you park the trailers. It was so shocking to me since I had just come off seven years on *Melrose Place* where sometimes we did not have a tech scout. Everyone knew the locations so we could have a one hour meeting at the office. And when we did go out, it was in a twelve passenger van with six to eight people in it full and we would scout for three to four hours. My first scout for *The X-Files* was a sixty passenger bus, with virtually every seat. We scouted from a steam plant in Long Beach all the way out to Palmdale and Lancaster. The scouting went from 7:00am and finished at 8:00pm. That was my introduction to *The X-Files* – it was pretty shocking. We also shot up at Paso Roso Ranch, near Vasquez rocks, near the edge of the 30 mile zone. For a couple of weeks we were shooting in the big water tanks, but that was also were the crew would report and be driven the rest of the way to the Lancaster/Palmdale location, except those that cheated and drove straight there and then magically appear when the vans arrived. You weren't supposed to transport yourself outside the 30 mile zone. Of the two weeks we spent filming this episode, ten days were up in the Lancaster, one out in the Long Beach area and then three days on stage. After spending five seasons up in Vancouver where things are usually wet and dark, I know that Chris and Frank were able to do a series of episodes that portrayed desert. I know for the first four or five episodes, everybody was drooling, because we were allowed to film out in the desert, something they could not do in Vancouver. They were able to get that whole mystery, the mythology, aliens landed years ago storyline. In the dessert, they could actually depict it, not just the interiors."

Location manager Mac Gordon talked to me about those giant water tanks for the episode. "We had to fill a huge water tank for *The Beginning*. It took a week to get it filled up and I spent the whole time on the phone with the people in charge of the pumps and the filtration system, making sure the dust that was blowing in did not get into the tanks. Two days before shooting began, the pumps broke and they could not replace it fast enough. I ordered round the clock water trucks to come and fill up and dump 2,500 gallons at a time. It cost us a little bit of money, but we were ready to film on time. When Kim pulled up, the water was clear, the right temperature, and full."

Shooting this episode was also educational for one underage actor. "When I went to LA to shoot *The Beginning* – my first trip outside of British Columbia – it was also my first time seeing boobs," shares Jeff Gulka. "Mitch Pileggi and I went to make up together and there was a sign on the trailer that said something like, 'Caution – Naked Girls Inside.' Before we entered Mitch told me, 'Well, here we go Jeff. This is your first time as a man."

6x02 Drive

Written by: Vince Gilligan
Directed by: Rob Bowman

Summary: While on a routine assignment Mulder and Scully see a news report, which catches their interest. The agents decide to investigate and soon Mulder finds himself in a car heading west with Patrick Crump. Slowing down or changing direction will cause the man's head to explode. Scully figures out that low frequency radio waves from a military antenna is the cause and needs to insert a large needle into his inner ear to relieve pressure. However, when Mulder reaches the Pacific coast, unable to go further west, it is already too late.

Location manager Mac Gordon talked to me about filming on location in the rural city of Acton for *Drive*. "In the early part of the season, we attracted a crowd and those people were a security concern since David and Gillian just attracted that. We never advertised where we were, nor did we advertise the name of the show on the crew signs. We would never ever, ever, ever, put anything 'X-Fillian' on the sign because (A) it would be gone in two seconds and (B) we didn't want that kind of attractor. Despite that, certain specialized individuals were savvy enough to know where we were and who we were. I'm usually the first person on location; I'm there before the trucks to make sure the gates are open and stuff. On one occasion I found two women who had flown in from the East Coast and they were waiting for us. They had never met; only chatted online and agreed to meet in L.A. to go watch a shoot. They lucked out because David's wife was expecting a baby any minute and he kept walking past them to get a signal for his cell phone. There was a lot of Duchovny time for them and most people didn't get that. The girls were respectful, and I admired their determination and dedication. We had a good security team and our policy was usually to befriend the fans, since they were there so often, and try to meet them and size them up to see if they were a little spooky or just serious fans."

Crew sign from Drive. Photo by Joy Krone.

"When we were on the set of *Drive*, we were excited because we found our first live filming location of our favorite television show," shares friends Joy Krone and Adrienne Doucette. "The first thing that we were told was that it was second unit filming, which is typically the teaser. Then we were introduced to Mac Gordon, the Location Manager. He asked us why we were there, and we told him that we were fans, loved the production quality of the show and were really interested in observing the filmmaking process. He told us that there would be no main actors there, no stunts or exciting things to see but we were welcome to hang around and watch. We respectfully observed from the sidelines for many hours and from time to time, various crew members would come by and share tidbits about the show with us. We were invited inside the location of Tom's house, given a tour of the set, and the man who owned Mr. Virgil Noke's house used in filming took us around his property. They were very kind to us. At the end of the night, Mac was kind enough to tell us that future filming would take place on the Queen Mary in Long Beach."

The back of Mr. Nokes place in *Drive*. Photo by Adrienne Doucette.

6x03 Triangle

Written by: Chris Carter
Directed by: Chris Carter
Summary: Mulder finds himself stuck in 1939 after he seeks out a WWII luxury liner in the Bermuda triangle. There is chaos onboard as German Nazis have boarded the ship looking for a weapon. Meanwhile, The Lone Gunmen and Scully are trying to locate Mulder, but when they finally arrive at the location they find nothing but a ghost ship. Before jumping over board, Mulder manages to convince 1939-Scully to make sure the ship turns around and goes back into the triangle. He is later picked up out of the sea, back in present day.

Queen Mary
1126 Queens Hwy
Long Beach, Ca

"Directing episodes was perhaps the most fun I had on the series, like *Post Modern Prometheus* and *Triangle*," Chris informs me. "*Triangle* was an overly ambitious episode, and one that took a tremendous amount of extra planning, care, and extra work for everyone involved," continues Chris. "It was a chance to do something that we had never done before, and I don't think that was ever done before on series television because it was such a gamble. Long, long, single takes, a lot of rehearsal, a lot of, ultimately, very careful camera work and focus pulling. David Luckenbach was for me a co-director on this episode. The camera needed to be a character; looking back and forth; anticipating the dialogue; pushing in and keeping the framing interesting. It was fun, but in the most intense way."

"I had seen an MTV video by the band Semisonic called *Closing Time*," adds Chris. "I loved that video and I actually got to meet those guys right around that time. It was a clever use of people moving through the split screen so that, for me, was an inspiration for the scene where both Scully's pass by one another in the same corridor and have a sense of one another. In the case of *Triangle*, the story lent itself to that kind of storytelling, I think, because of the different periods of time, and in *Improbable*, it was such a wacky episode; it required tricks with the split screen."

An episode like *Triangle* allowed the cast to break out of their character's comfort zone and try their hand at a new, or in one case, forgotten, language. "When they gave me my German lines, I told them it didn't make any sense, nor does it pertain to the scene in general," shares Mitch Pileggi. "I asked them if I could come up with something else, and I was able to come up with something else. I went to school in Germany for a couple of years and my German was pretty good, but now it has almost receded from my memory. I think I remember how to count to ten at this point in my life."

"Speaking German was a challenge," William B. Davis informs me. "I was quite proud of my German. People who didn't speak German were asking me, 'Gee, do you speak German? Wow that sounds really good.' And [when asked], the people who really did speak German said, 'I really don't even want to say.' So I guess my German wasn't as good as I thought it was!"

The soundtrack to *Triangle* has been a fan favorite since it aired. Mark Snow shares the evolution of this episode's particular score. "A version of Benny Goodman was in the temp music and they said to me this works great; can you get close to it?" says Mark. "*Triangle* was creative and amazing and totally fun for me to really get out of *The X-Files* musically and dabble into Big Band, which my dad was a part of. He was in one of those Benny Goodman bands as a drummer so I had that music floating around the house when I was a kid."

"I wish we would have done this episode back in Season Three," Bill Roe tells me. "This was the second episode that I shot. We never knew the titles of the episodes when we shot them; it was always episode 6x03 or Untitled. The episodes were given names much later, after we were done shooting. I would say 80% of the shows titles we never knew what they were. I think Chris wanted it done that way because he didn't want the names getting out. This was also the first time Chris and I had worked together with him being a director. To this day, it's probably one of the biggest episodes we have ever done. Every shot was 4 minutes, which was the length of the magazine in the film. We did two shots a day and then say goodnight. It was very difficult. We were on the Queen Mary for a week and I remember looking down at the parking lot of the Queen Mary and seeing a whole parking lot full of forty foot trailers. There must have been thirty of them. I remember thinking to myself, 'This is only my second episode. Oh my gosh, what have I gotten myself into?' I had a great crew and with the help of all those people, we were able to figure it all out. We had BB lights, which are lights used at night to resemble moon-light in large areas. When you're on the Queen Mary at night, there is this sodium-mercury vapor that spills onto the deck because it lights the parking lot. We had to turn all those parking lights off because we didn't want the orange and green light spilling into the scene. It was very expensive just to light the parking lot with these BB lights so the crew could work."

Side view if the Queen Mary, Long Beach, Ca. Photo by Erica Fraga

"When we were on the Queen Mary, we sat on the ship's deck and played cards, carefully observing our surroundings," report Joy and Adrienne Together. "We saw many people come and go, including stunt men and background actors in period costume. We were entertained by security guards telling curious passersby that they were filming a milk commercial in order to deter people from staying. At one point, there was a large gathering of people taking pictures of sopping wet David Duchovny after Nazi soldiers pulled him out of the water. This necessitated the removal of numerous observers by an Assistant

Director, but fortunately, we were on the sidelines and permitted to stay. One of the other fortunate observers, Little Star, joined in our card game (and is still our good friend to this day). At one point, while the Lone Gunmen were waiting to go on set, they came over and asked us about our card game. They engaged us in conversation, watched our game for a while and even took pictures with us. The next day, we met the very approachable and pleasant Chris Owens. He took us over to the ship's milkshake shop, where we had milkshakes together. He even signed our cups when we were done. Unfortunately, one of the cups later became a chewing toy for my cat and was destroyed. We learned from then on to preserve all treasured artifacts in glass cases (see picture of surviving cup.) Regardless of the ill-mannered behavior of my cat, we had amazing experience on the *Triangle* set."

Cup signed by Chris Owens. Photo by Adrienne Doucette.

Editor's Note: A trip to the Queen Mary is a must not just for any *X-Files* fan, but also for any history buff. There are guided tours of the ship and traveling exhibits on display. In addition, a wonderful Halloween event takes place every October, where the ship is turned into one big haunted maze. Check online for information on price and hours of operation.

6x04 Dreamland 1

Written by: Vince Gilligan, John Shiban, Frank Spotnitz
Directed by: Kim Manners
Summary: The agents are on their way to meet a source at Area 51 when a tear in the space-time continuum makes Mulder switch bodies with Man In Black, Morris Fletcher. A malfunctioning aircraft appears to be the cause of the tear. Morris is enjoying his new life as an FBI agent while Mulder is desperately trying to get things back to normal - and to convince Scully that her partner is not who she thinks he is. Mulder steals the plane's flight data recorder to prove his story, but is arrested after Morris sets him up.

Gas Station (where Mulder/Morris is arrested)
Chevron Gas
6900 S. Centinela Ave.
Culver City, Ca
***This location was also used in *Brand X*

Author's Note: A word to the fans reading this book; don't bother looking for the rural gas station where the penny/dime combination coin was found in the episode. According to Mac Gordon, that location was built by stage hands up in Lancaster, blown up for the show, and then all traces removed when filming was completed.

6x05 Dreamland 2

Written by: Vince Gillian, John Shiban, Frank Spotnitz
Directed by: Michael Watkins
Summary: Mulder is released after it is discovered that the flight data recorder was fake. He convinces the Men In Black that he did it to expose the security leak. They eventually get the real recorder to The Lone Gunmen, but their analysis concludes that what happened was a random event and is impossible to recreate. Luckily, the rift in the space-time continuum starts reversing on its own and soon everything is back to normal.

Little A'le'Inn
Club Ed Movie Ranch
42848 150th St.
Lancaster, Ca

"I was out in the LA area on vacation with my family and after checking the EIDC film websites, my friend and I went down to Encino the next morning," reveals fan Kathleen Keegan. "We saw the production trucks in a residential area, and we weren't sure this was the right place. We saw a security guard and we were going to go up to him and ask if this was *The X-Files* shoot, but before we could do that, we saw a big black SUV come slowly around the corner and there's David sitting in the front passenger seat. My friend and I looked at each other and said, 'I guess we're in the right spot!' They were filming scenes at Morris Fletcher's house. They did some scenes outside and some scenes inside. Everybody could not have been any nicer to us. They were so excited that we were there to watch them; they made us feel super welcome. They checked to make sure we were okay, they showed us where to stand to get the best views, and to be out of the cameras way; offered us water and food throughout the course of the day. They offered us the use of their facilities; they invited us to sit down at lunch with the crew. We talked to David a couple of times that way and he was funny because they had some director's chairs set up on the driveway of Morris Fletcher's house. The cul-de-sac is not very big, and I don't know what it is about his voice; it's soft, yet it carries. No matter where he was on street, you could hear him talking. He was not talking very loudly, but you can hear him talking to the hair and make-up people and he was telling them some stories; I forget what they were now. When he was called to set, he turns around and tells the folks, 'Now don't let me forget where I left off.' He went to film the scene where Mulder, as Fletcher, was being kicked out of his house. He's picking stuff up that's being thrown at him, and placing into a U-Haul. We were there for about 11 hours because we were having such a good time with everyone there. It was amazing."

"Since they filmed on a weekday, most of the homeowners were away at work so it was really quiet during the day except for the house that was directly across the street," continues Kathleen. "It had a big dog in the backyard behind a fence and he barked incessantly at everyone milling around on the street. At one point in time he began to interfere with filming and they threw some peanut butter sandwiches over the fence to shut the dog up. That worked for maybe ten, twenty minutes, and the dog started up again. This was right before their lunch break so they threw a lot of beef tenderloin over the fence at the dog. The dog ate it all up and must have gone to sleep right after that because we never heard from him after that."

"A little bit later on in the afternoon, this red, beat up, pick-up truck comes pulling down the street," says Kathleen. "The crew is trying to get him to stop coming down the street because he has no muffler and his truck is making this 'BOOM - BOOM - BOOM' sound as he is coming down the street. People are yelling 'Stop him!" and everyone is trying to talk to him and it's then that they realize it's someone's gardener, who happens not to speak English very well. So, then they were yelling for someone who speaks Spanish to stop the poor guy. It was one interruption after another but the crew was just hysterical with laughter.

Nothing really spectacular happened; it was just a nice, fun, relaxing day. And, of all the time that I have been on set after that, nothing has every surpassed that day since everyone was having such a great time and made us feel really welcome."

6x08 How The Ghosts Stole Christmas

Written by: Chris Carter
Directed by: Chris Carter
Summary: It's Christmas Eve and the agents are staking out an old house which, every year on this day, is haunted by the ghosts of star-crossed lovers Maurice and Lydia. As Mulder and Scully enter the house, the ghosts, who also turns out to be hobby psychologists, start having their fun. Their aim is to get another double murder so the house gets put back into the tourist books. Although the ghosts manage to make the agents believe they've both been shot by their partner, Mulder figures out it was all in their heads and they eventually escape unharmed.

Haunted Mansion
Newhall Mansion
829 N. Park St.
Piru, Ca

Being a fan of the series, I asked Chris Carter to shed some light on the enigmatic Christmas gifts Mulder and Scully give to each other at the end of the episode. In true fashion, Chris notifies me that "I won't tell you what they got each other at the end of the episode, but I will say that they were very personalized gifts."

Sorry guys, I tried.

Editor's Note: This location is a bit of a drive from Los Angeles, but completely worth it. Where most of the locations have changed throughout the years, this house looks very much the way it did in the episode, so much so that on our scouting trip the mere sight of this house induced *many* squeals in the car.

6x07 Rain King

Written by: Jeffrey Bell
Directed by: Kim Manners
Summary: Mulder and Scully head to Kroner, Kansas to investigate a man suspected of causing the drought so he can charge people for making it rain. Kroner has been at the center of many bizarre weather conditions, however it turns out that it is not The Rain King who is causing it but rather the weather man at the local TV station. His unexpressed emotions are manifesting themselves in the weather and not until he finally manages to express his love for his best friend (with a little help from the FBI) does the weather return to normal.

Kroner High School Gym
Broadway Gymnastics School
5433 Beethoven St.
Los Angeles, Ca

Cow Motel
Spunelli Motel
12117 Sierra Hwy
Santa Clarita, Ca

TV Station
KLCS-TV
1061 W. Temple St.
Los Angeles, Ca

"I started off as a Unit Production Manager and a First Assistant Director for the second unit – which is as big as the main unit- in my first season with *The X-Files*," Harry Bring shares with me. "Whenever I think back to my time on the set, which I missed once I was promoted to Producer, *The Rain King* is still my all time favorite episode to this day. It's my favorite because of the premise and how we shut down Temple Highway one night and manufactured rain, which turned into hail, into heart shaped hail, and then a car crash. There was this four mile stretch of defunct highway that parallels Highway 5 freeway, out past Castaic. We took this highway over for a night of filming, which took place in the colder months, so we had a longer night. And we needed every second of it. Thank God it was Kim shooting it because we never would have gotten it down in one night. We had this forty foot truck, filled with blocks of ice, with a wood chipper shooting ice; from tiny to coarse to big over this four mile run, after having a whole lot of rain. It was surreal and it was such a challenge to do and we did it. Even though it was several shows into my first season, that's when I realized I was part of something very special and it would replace all the other shows that I ever worked on that I loved."

"Kim knows his way around the block, will turn to people like me and ask 'what's the closest we can get to this idea?' and we kind of go from there," reveals Mac Gordon. "I will say that on *The X-Files* more often than not, we somehow always managed to bend it to our will and find the right locations, and find houses, to let us dig up their backyard to have a dead baby in it, just crazy stuff. Or we'll go to a little motel and tell the owner, 'We want to shoot here, but by the way, we want to punch a hole in the roof so a cow can fly through it. Is that ok?' After the initial shock wears off, they are usually okay with it. In fact, I had to go find the owner of some land very near the motel where we put the cow through the roof. I had to ask if it was okay if we graded a runway on their property and amazingly they were amenable to it and we did it. We graded a dirt runway, flew a plane, shot a scene there, and then flew the plane out again."

6x10 S.R. 819

Written by: John Shiban
Directed by: Daniel Sackheim
Summary: Skinner becomes very ill after being poisoned and has 24 hours to live. Mulder and Scully find that he became a target because he was doing a security check on a proposed senate bill regarding nanotechnology. Skinner's blood is now full of nanites, which can be remotely controlled to block his arteries by none other than Alex Krycek.

In addition to forgetting his German, Mitch Pileggi talked to me about his character on *S.R. 819*, and how different it was to play A.D. Skinner. "This episode was fun for me since I boxed in college, and I think that is why they threw that in," laughs Mitch. "In *S.R. 819* I kept tagging the boxer I was sparring with, and I'm pretty good about on screen fights and not hitting other people, but when you have big gloves on, sometimes you can't tell how hard you're hitting and I got a pretty good punch in. At one point my opponent yelled out, 'Mitch keeps hitting me!' And I would yell back, 'I'm sorry!' He was a pretty big guy, so to hear him say that was hilarious".

"The nanites – not so much fun," bellows Mitch. "There were bladders involved; tubes going up my arms; I had to push these air bags to make different things pulse. It took a long time to put it on and it took a long time while it was on to maintain it; to keep it functioning. I'm trying to act, trying to say dialogue, but I have to remember that I have to keep pumping these bulbs in my hand. It was not my favorite part of the show and after a few episodes with this get up, at one point I went to Frank and told him I didn't like it so much anymore and could we solve this nano problem. They did get rid of it, thank God. It was actually the hardest thing I had to do on the show."

"Anytime I was able to get out from behind that desk, take the suit and tie off, other than the time I paraded around in my underwear in

Season 4, was a lot of fun," recalls Mitch. "Actually I did something goofy for *Zero Sum*. Right before one of the takes, I had wardrobe give me a bra and panty set. I came down the staircase in women's underwear. It was not a pretty picture, believe me, and I'm glad it did not end up in *TV Guide*. Rob Bowman's little brother Steven was on set, his first time visiting the set, and I think I traumatized him. He still talks about this 6'2" bald man in bra and panties to this day."

"I remember this day where I had gone on my shoot the day before and the head of production told me I was being punished for going long and was taking out two hours from my shoot the next day," reminisces producer/director Dan Sackheim. "I remember thinking, 'How am I going to do this?' It was a challenging day, since we had the boxing scene and a trip to the hospital. They even sent a junior executive from the studio to stay on the set and watch me, to make sure I did not go over. Somehow I managed to shoot a twelve hour day in ten hours, with something like four minutes to spare. I remember this time challenge very fondly, because I was actually able to meet the challenge, despite it being absolutely terrifying and exhilarating at the same time. *S.R. 819* was one of the best episodes I did for this reason."

6x09 Tithonus

Written by: Vince Gilligan
Directed by: Michael Watkins
Summary: Scully is partnered with a new agent and is sent to investigate a crime scene photographer, Alfred Fellig, who appears to have more to do with several murders than just taking the pictures. Fellig wants to take a photo of death itself so that he himself, now at the age of 149, finally can die. Scully's new partner accidentally shoots her as he tries to arrest Fellig, but the photographer dies instead of her, leaving us wondering if Scully is now immortal.

"You're not always shooting in the most desirable areas," warns Harry Bring. "You are shooting alleys or dank areas and locations with a lot of character and are probably a hundred years old, or the neighborhood is not too good. We always had to have extra security because we were always getting hit up. If you did not have every truck monitored, you would lose stuff from theft or be disturbed by the junkies or alcoholics. Crowd control was always an issue, friendly or foe. Sometimes there would be fifty guys a few blocks away, local store owners, who would come down and say that we were affecting their business and want a pay off. I mean, their stores would be blocks from where our activity was. A lot of other productions, especially commercials, would succumb and pay everybody who thinks they need reimbursement or compensation."

6x12 One Son

Written by: Chris Carter & Frank Spotnitz
Directed by: Rob Bowman
Summary: Mulder, Scully and Cassandra are taken into quarantine on Diana Fowley's orders. Scully is highly suspicious of her motives and suggests it was all staged to kidnap Cassandra. In an attempt to save themselves, the Consortium wants to hand over Cassandra to the aliens. Jeffrey Spender finally realizes the extent of the conspiracy and makes sure that Mulder and Scully are put back on the X-Files.

Basketball Gym
J. Manuel Presbyterian Church
3300 Wilshire Blvd.
Los Angeles, Ca

Consortium Hangar
Marine Corps Air Station
Newport Freeway and Red Hill Ave
Tustin, Ca

6x14 Agua Mala

Written by: David Amann
Directed by: Rob Bowman
Summary: The original X-Files agent, Arthur Dales, brings Mulder and Scully down to Florida to look into the disappearance of a family who Dales suspects has been killed by a sea monster. The agents arrive in the middle of a hurricane and are forced to seek shelter in an apartment building where they encounter the creature which has entered the building's plumbing through a backwash of seawater.

"*Agua Mala* was one of my favorite episodes, and it was one of my first episodes with Rob," Bill Roe says. "I won the ASC Cinematography awards that year. *Agua Mala* was a whole different way of lighting that I had never done before. Rob and I discussed the episode and we did everything with practical lights. It was very cool how we staged the light, and that is one thing Rob is good at. He understands light, he loves light, and he works his shows around the light. *Agua Mala* is a good example of that."

"What's fun for me was trying to tell the story through scene design," adds Rob Bowman. "We like to go to the edge of our capabilities in terms of what we can do in a day. And figuring out what those essential action moments were so that you could accomplish a shot. I mean, we're shooting Russian's on horses, cars going over cliffs, and alien lights coming through trees. You can be standing in 200 mile an hour hurricane force winds and maintaining deep focus. It was self inflicted misery on set for *Agua Mala*, but it was a remarkable episode because I wanted funny, and at times life threatening. Mixing those tones was a challenge, but we had a fun time doing this 'bottle' show, which means we were in one place and we had to entertain the audience for an hour. So we had to find ways to keep it interesting; keep it moving to create escalation; room changes within a scene sequence so it feels like you're telling a story. I had such a great time doing that; I can't believe it. It was a real fun thing for me to do since that's what my hero's did. Working on the show was the easiest and most fun thing to do. It was arduous, but I enjoyed it."

"We had to black out sixteen square blocks of Long beach, to make it look like a storm had knocked down all the power," Ilt Jones tells me. "We had to switch off every light in every house, in every building. We had to make it rain throughout the whole area and we only had a few days to pull it off. And this was for a television show, not a feature. That was one of the great things about the show; it was very high speed and great training for the features I worked on, like both *Transformers* films and *Hancock*."

Author's Note: When I went out to find this location in Long Beach, I discovered that the beach side property that was the Breakers Condominium in the episode was torn down, and replaced with a whole new street and development. Alas, nothing resembles the 3 story apartment complex that once stood there.

6x15 Monday

Written by: Vince Gilligan & John Shiban
Directed by: Kim Manners
Summary: Mulder is having a really bad day which ends with himself and Scully being blown up inside a bank during a robbery. Until he wakes up the next day and finds the same thing happening again. And again, and again. The bank robber's girlfriend, Pam, is the only one who knows what is going on and is desperately trying to convince Mulder of it, day after day. Mulder eventually makes himself remember and is able to break the cycle by having Scully bring Pam into the bank to stop the robbery.

Craddock and Maine Bank
Farmers and Merchant Bank
401 S. Main St.
Los Angeles, Ca

"When we were setting up for our exterior bank work leading up to the explosion, one day was normal photography, the comings and goings of our characters, and the second day was when we blew out the windows," describes Harry Bring. "Basically we were a two camera show and on this day we had seven cameras and two remote cameras. On explosion day it took three hours to get the front of the bank ready and I was walking around the masses of people with my hand farter and just nailing people. I acted like I was not with the crew, but a 'looky-loo' and nailing folks left and right. Kim could not concentrate because all he wanted to do was watch me at work. The reactions I got ranged from thoroughly disgusted to laughing so hard they were almost wetting their pants, especially later on when they found out it was a gag. We had this one female security guard that stood by the A camera the whole time, from rehearsal to shoot day. Kim could not concentrate because she was literally on the ground, rolling around the street, laughing. Thankfully traffic was all shut down. Sometimes Kim would tell me, when we shot different locations and I was not readily available, to bring my hand farter since we were in a great location. He loved it and he would tell me who to go nail and then sit back and watch their reactions."

"It took the crew a good portion of the week to dress the bank so it was ready to go, like put in the special windows that had break-a-way glass for the explosions;" expresses Kathleen Keegan. "I was there with some fans from X-Philes Anonymous (XPA) group and we started to talk to the crew along the way and we found out when they were actually going to start filming there and it just so happened that it was going to be the day that we were leaving. The whole group changed their flights so we could be there for the filming. I had also heard from another XPA member that the night before the Golden Globes they had filmed the water bed scene with David in his little yellow jammy bottoms. Soaking wet. With no underwear on. And walking around the set all day long; not a care in the world. She said that she didn't see anything and David was already gone by the time she arrived on set, but the female crew was still buzzing when she arrived."

"We spent the better portion of the day there and the crew was wonderful again," continues Kathleen. "We parked in a parking garage down the corner and we're walking up the street where the bank is when we see someone who looks like Mulder walking down the street towards us. The other people in my group were like, 'Oh my God, here comes David!' and I looked over at him and told the group that it was not David, but Steve his stunt double. He was still a good block and a half away but I could tell by the walk that it wasn't him. We stood on the corner and base camp was another block or so down on the other corner. We saw a homeless guy come walking around the corner and vomit all over the sidewalk near the bank. We called over Lee, the Unit Production Manager, and told him he might want to get rid of that. The craft services woman came out and poured something over it and then washed the sidewalk down. There was also a peel-n-stick plaque that they had put up on the side of the building, which showed the fake address. At one point, the letters began to fall off so we picked them up and gave them to Lee. Well, Lee is a short little guy and he couldn't get them back up on the building. One of the guys I was with was really tall, so he gave Lee a boost on his hands so Lee could stand on them and place them back on the building. We never got a chance to speak to Kim, but I remember his 'Penguin Walk' on that day as he hustled back and forth across the street. In addition to being a firecracker, Kim was bow legged and he had this distinctive walk that the cast and crew would imitate, which I think is featured in one of the season's blooper reels. The faster Kim went, the funnier his walk became."

"We're all standing and talking to ourselves and there was this group of little giggling fifteen-year old girls that came over to us," carries on Kathleen. "They were asking us questions and all. I told them that the crew would be really cool to them if they didn't take any cameras out, do what they were told to do, be courteous, respectful, nice, and they will let you hang out as long as you want and you'll be treated really well. We told them not to make a scene because if they get kicked out, chances are we would as well. I happened to be facing the direction of base camp and I see David walking down the street towards the set. This was the day they filmed David getting shot in the bank. Most people that were walking from base camp cut across the street, closer to the bank. Not David. He purposely crossed the street on his side, and then crossed 4th St. so he had to walk through our little crowd. As he did that, he looks at each and every one of us, and tells us, 'Good morning girls'. The younger girls started giggling and making a fuss, and as David is leaving he starts chuckling to himself. We were able to watch them film inside the bank by looking into the side windows, so that was really cool. At the end of the night we asked to take pictures and get autographs, and David posed for a group shot in his suit, trench coat, and fake blood all over the shirt. He pulls his trench coat closer to his body and tells me, 'I don't want to get any on you.' I turn to look at him and reply, 'You could rub it all over me and I wouldn't care!' He started laughing at that."

6x13 Arcadia

Written by: Daniel Arkin
Directed by: Michael Watkins
Summary: Mulder and Scully go undercover as a married couple to investigate the disappearance of several homeowners in a seemingly perfect neighborhood.

During my interviews, I discovered that one episode, the fan favorite 6x15 *Arcadia,* almost never made it to television due to the Tulpa character – a monster created from garbage - in this Monster-Of-The-Week episode. "A Production Assistant told us that the production was struggling to reconstruct the monster in *Arcadia* so that the quality of the episode's special effects would be acceptable for air," according to fans Adrienne Doucette and Joy Krone. "Thankfully, the monster was successfully refurbished and the episode aired!"

David Duchovny confirms that the Tulpa was the main hindrance in the episode. "They made the set dark enough so the audience never got a look at the creature. Michael Watkins had the best line about the monster when he said the creature looked like the guy fucked Mrs. Butterworth."

"I have to be honest with you, this was probably my most uncomfortable experience," confides Michael Watkins. "I called [the monster] Fecal Fred and it was just terrible. I don't want to be disparaging here, but the creators put out 22-26 shows a season. Stuff just happens. And you can't do a perfect show every single time. Helga, the script person up here in Canada, saw the show and called me and we were laughing. There is always a clunker every single year. It's like playing Hearts, the card game. I had a hell of a time embracing it and you fought to make it better. Then David comes out wearing a pink polo shirt and the monster comes out looking like a melted donut. It was really tough and we kept going. I was bothered about having to do it, but I see on different lists that people still talk about it so I guess it served some purpose for them."

"Arcadia was filmed in West Lake Village," Mac Gordon shares with me. "We secured a gated community and we talked some young couple into not only letting us shoot in their house before Christmas, but we went away for two weeks, and then we came back to shoot after Christmas. In the course of that time we had dug up their entire front yard and the hole stayed there for a while. In fact, it was an ordeal to repair when we were done because we had to compress the ground back. The couple was put out a little bit by us, but they didn't mind too much since they were paid handsomely. Generally people were excited of a show of that stature [in their neighborhood]. I think the only time we got in trouble was some of the night work. We had to light up the whole neighborhood and part of my job was to go knock on doors and ask people if we could put lights into their backyard and stuff like that. By and large, people were okay with us. We put almost all of our big equipment outside the gated community. We were always mindful to try not to be too much of a pain in the ass."

6x16 Alpha

Written by: Jeffrey Bell
Directed by: Peter Markle
Summary: An Asian dog believed to be extinct, a Wanshang Dhole, is on the loose after killing two people from the ship on which it was transported. Several other people die after being attacked and Mulder seeks help from an expert in dog behavior he's met online.

Authors Note: Trying to find Karen's House was an adventure for my companions and I. After driving through the winding roads of Calabasas, we arrived at a dead end street in a heavily wooded residential area. At first, we could not find Karen's house. We had a general idea of where it was after reviewing the DVD's and we knew the street it was on. After several passes – and inquisitive stares from the locals – we found the house, tucked away down a private road. Taking the correct action, we decided not to trespass and began making dinner plans. Luckily we stayed in the car because at that very moment, a neighbor's dog – a very angry neighbor's dog – ran out of the neighbor's yard and tried to jump into my half open window.

6x17 Trevor

Written by: Jim Guttridge & Ken Hawryliw
Directed by: Rob Bowman

Summary: A prison inmate, Pinker Rawls, goes missing when the prison is hit by a tornado. Instead of dying he picks up the ability to walk through solid objects. Mulder and Scully suspect Rawls has gone looking for the money from the robbery which sent him behind bars, but in reality he's looking for his son.

Mini Mart
Luckey's Liquor, Deli, and Market
9680 1/2 Sunland Blvd
Los Angeles, Ca

6x18 Milagro

Written by: Chris Carter, Frank Spotnitz, and John Shiban
Directed by: Kim Manners
Summary: Scully has a secret admirer: Mulder's new neighbor Phillip Padgett. He's a writer but has imagined his book so well that the character comes to life and the murders he describes actually happen. Padgett's having a hard time coming up with an ending, but with a little help from his main character he realizes that Scully, an important character in his book, must die.

Milagro Church
First Congregational Church of Los Angeles
540 S. Commonwealth Ave.
Los Angeles, Ca

Mountain View Cemetery
2400 N. Fair Oaks Dr.
Altadena, CA
***This site was also utilized in *Millennium*

Milagro is arguably one of the most beautifully written and poignant episodes of Season 6. Kim's direction is magnificent; Scully's femininity, described through the eyes of a voyeur -an outsider- is superbly reflected in Gillian Anderson's acting.

"*Milagro* took me by surprise," recalls Mark Snow. "When I first saw the Pilot, both David and Gillian were so young, almost pubescent compared to where they are now. To see them change and grow through the years was pretty great. You saw Gillian change into this real powerful woman, but still soft and feminine and dramatically beautiful."

"One of my friends, Heather, who I have lost contact with, was watching the second unit film in the cemetery," says Adrienne Doucette. "Kim saw them and engaged Heather and her friend in a conversation about the episode and what was going on with the episode. They ended up staying with him for a long time and when they were done, Kim gave them each a hug. When she told us that story, it sounded like he was so cool. Unfortunately, my friend Joy and I never had that experience."

6x20 The Unnatural

Written by: David Duchovny
Directed by: David Duchovny
Summary: When the Alien Bounty Hunter shows up in a photo with Arthur Dales and a 1947 baseball team, Mulder tracks him down to hear the story. Arthur Dales, brother of X-Files veteran Arthur Dales, was a cop in Roswell assigned to protect Negro League star Josh Exley. He was an alien who stayed behind on earth because he fell in love with baseball and wishes to live his life as a human.

Old Time Baseball Park
Jay Littleton Baseball Field
900 N. Grove Ave.
Ontario, Ca

Played as Scully's birthday gift
Cheviot Hills Park
2551 Motor Ave.
Los Angeles, Ca
***This park was used again in *Three Words* and *Lord of the Flies*.

The old time baseball park from *The Unnatural*. Photo by Erica Fraga.

David Duchovny made his directorial debut near the end of Season 6 with *The Unnatural* 6x20. *The Unnatural* was funny, exciting, and compelling as the character of Arthur Dales tells the story of Negro league player Josh Exley to Agent Fox Mulder. David shared the following regarding his inspiration for the show.

"Before I shot *The Unnatural*, I did a walk through with Kim of my sets and scenes and told him what I was thinking of," shares David Duchovny. "The big home run race between Mark McGuire and Sammy Sosa was going on that year and there was an article in *LA Times* about this minor league player who had hit 70 home runs and it all came together at that point. I had the idea [from that], I certainly knew Mulder's voice and just went from there."

"This was one of the most fun times we ever had on a television show," Bill Roe tells me about his time on *The Unnatural*. "I'm a big sports guy so going back in time and coming up with this period idea was great. We had a lot of fun, but we had a lot of problems in terms of weather, but we got through it all. When it was all over, we played baseball together. There was always a ball on the set, whether it was a baseball or football, or just hanging out; we always did sports."

Regarding *The Unnatural*, "I am proud of me as a producer and I never left this show," evokes Michael Watkins. "I was with it every instant of the day. I carved a baseball field out of a mountain. Darrin McGavin had a stroke after two days and we had to re-hire. I had a first time writer/director and I never left his side. That was a big show for us. We were on everybody's radar. I think they anticipated David not succeeding and it was very daunting for David. I love David for showing up; I thought his writing was spectacular. I would catch a plane every night when we were in Ontario, and I had to fly to Vegas because they were shooting all night in Vegas and I would work all night with the other crew, and then I flew back and worked all day with David. I did that for four of five straight days. We never lost a day in shooting; we were always on schedule. I found ways to do it, David was pliable, and the actors were pliable. I'm really proud of that. We would stop at Gladstone's on the way home and have a beer and talk about the show. I had a friend there, as well as somebody I worked with. It was a really good time for me then. It was one of the really joyous times for me, and David was very generous after that show. It was great."

"I was a freshman in high school and my best friend's mom found out from a coworker that *The X-Files* was filming in Ontario," reminisces Courtney Smith. "We hopped into the car Monday night and we drove to the set. We walk up to the edge of the baseball field, and we see that they are filming. We look really close and we see David Duchovny walking around. It was then that we realized that this was the episode he was directing, which had been talked about for a really long time. As we're watching, a production assistant (PA) comes up to us and tells us, 'You know what, if you come back tomorrow around 10 o'clock, we can probably get you on set, we can probably get you in the episode because they're always looking for extras.' [My friend] and I go home that night very excited and then we realize that we have standardized testing tomorrow morning. My Mom and my best friend's Mom write us notes, saying that we have a doctor's appointment, which gets us out of class. We get picked up from school and we go over to the same PA from last night, who leads us over to the costume lady. She looks at my step-dad and tells him, 'All you need is a hat. Otherwise you look perfect.' Then she looks at me and my best friend and tells us that we need some costumes and then hands us some fun and flirty costumes from the 1930s which was really awesome."

"We walked into the actual baseball field, and we were going to watch them film," carries on Courtney. "The one scene that I remember very clearly, that they shot from the morning until about 2 or 3 that afternoon to get all the angles, was when Arthur Dales tackles Exley to the ground. Afterwards we broke for lunch. There was a raffle being held, and when we were given our Subway sandwiches, we were given a raffle ticket. Some of the prizes were the *Fight the Future* soundtrack and copies of the movie. The biggest prize was a *Fight the Future* movie poster autographed by David Duchovny. I was the fan who won it. I was very excited and it's in my living room to this day."

"After lunch, we went back to the set and they were going to film reaction shots of the crowd," keeps on Courtney. "David took a microphone and walked back and forth in front of us. He told us, 'Okay, I'm going to give you guys some direction and I want you to respond to what I'm saying.' The cameras were set up and David would say things like, '*Your favorite batter is up at the plate and he just hit a home run.*

Everyone respond!' and *'Okay, alright, alright, your favorite batter is at the plate and he just struck out. How do you respond?'*, and *'Okay, your favorite player just got hit by a ball.'* Once the reaction shots were done, they called it a wrap. Now, in order [for FOX] to get their costumes back from the extras, they had these shirts made up that said *The Unnatural* on the front and *The X-Files* on the back and it was done in old time style writing. As we were leaving the set, the same PA that had got us on set, told us, 'Just a heads up. They are doing some night filming inside, and if you want to wait at this gate, and if you're patient and quiet, David might come outside to sign autographs and take pictures for about half an hour.' We waited quietly and respectfully and then gate opened up and David Duchovny walks out. He was so wonderful. He signed autographs, took pictures, answered questions, and was just really great. He was there for about 45 minutes to an hour, and then went back in for more filming. At that point the set was cleared of all extras and a month later my episode came on T.V."

6x19 Three of a Kind

Written by: Vince Gilligan & John Shiban
Directed by: Bryan Spicer
Summary:___The Lone Gunmen attend a Las Vegas convention to catch the scoop on what the government is up to when they run into Susanne Modeski. Her life is in danger after she helped develop a drug for the government which makes anyone injected with it susceptible to mind control and brainwashing, something which both Scully and Langly get to experience. However, the Gunmen manage to save Modeski's life and can return home with another story for their own newspaper.

Def-Con Convention
The Century Plaza Hyatt Regency Hotel
2025 Ave of the Stars
Los Angeles, Ca
***Room # 1066 Susan Modeski

"I had an actor crisis on *Three of a Kind* because for years I had been playing Byers as a married man, wearing my own wedding ring in the part," shares Bruce Harwood. "It turned out that the writers and producers had never noticed my wedding ring, so in *Three of a Kind* they'd written me as unmarried and put a whole wedding ring thing into the script. I panicked because Byers being married was a central tenet of my personal back story for him, and because I knew the Gunmen fans also knew Byers wore a ring. Eventually I just decided that Byers had been married, somewhere on the timeline between *Unusual Suspects* and the start of *The X-Files*, and his wife had divorced him very quickly, because he was never around, always at the office with Langly and Frohike, but he'd continued to wear his wedding ring for years out of misplaced loyalty. That is the kind of thing Byers would do."

"The only thing I remember about working in Vegas for *Three of a Kind* is that Tom and Dean had time off and went out on an all-night drinking party, and I had to go to bed to get up early and drive out to the cold, cold desert and stand in a blasting wind to shoot a dream sequence," continues Bruce. "When I came back that afternoon, the other two guys showed up talking about the great time they'd had the night before, and how much they enjoyed the massages they'd had before coming to work. Also, everybody else was winning on the slots and I kept losing. Vegas is not a fun place to be when you're working."

Three of a Kind was a unique episode for comedian Dean Haglund because the audience was able to see Langley brainwashed, and therefore very stoic and serious as he prepares to kill a convention go-er. "Well, it is funny you see," replies Dean. "All the years I was doing *The X-Files*, I thought I was being very stoic and serious as Langly, but people were laughing anyway. When it came time to be brainwashed, I just had no lines to say so it seemed like I was different. But it is the curse of being born funny, I guess. The hardest part was not flinching when they sprayed red blood in my face after the gun shot. They had to do that three times until I got it right!

Season Seven:

A Turning Point

Season Seven had many outstanding moments within the history of the show. Veteran cast members David Duchovny, Gillian Anderson and William B Davis all directed episodes. Fox Mulder finally learned the fate of his sister, Samantha; Dana Scully learned that she was pregnant. Shooting on location had both its perks and disadvantages. When the show traveled outside of the 30 mile zone to the San Bernardino Mountains to film *Requiem*, Kim found creative ways to take the show back to the look of Season One. Of course, time and budget were Kim's biggest enemies, but with the help of his beloved crew, the show came together. I asked the crew to share some of their favorite memories of Kim on the Big Bear shoot.

"Kim was an experienced director; he knew basically the same issues and problems that we would have in Southern California," Mac Gordon tells me. "That is partly the reason Kim had such a strong influence on some shows where we went. We went to Big Bear and he wanted it to be more going and more feeling and we could not do that in the L.A. based area so we went up there and that was wild time. I liked working with Kim and I remember him shooting the nights. My night would end at 11:00 pm; go back to the hotel; get some sleep; get up in the morning and go manage prepping. Kim and his team would just be coming in from the woods since they had been out all night. Somehow Kim convinced the hotel to open the bar at 7:00am. By 8:30am, when I'm ready to cruise out, there was a loud, raucous party going on in the hotel bar since that was their evening."

"Kim called me from [Big Bear] and he said he was getting hammered because the days are short and he was having trouble getting all the angles and image sizes that he wanted," says editor Heather MacDougal. "He asked me if I would blow up shots so that he would have medium close ups as well as tight close ups and any other image size changes that I thought would help him tell the story. Paul Rabwin got mad at me for doing that, but of course I was happy to help Kim anyway I could. We had worked together on the other 10 episodes so he did trust my judgment. Kim knew what he was doing and he knew he didn't have enough time to do the job with the grace that he wanted it to have, so he used me as a time-saving tool. It would have taken him extra hours on the set to get all the image sizes he wanted and he didn't have that time, so he set things up the way he wanted them, knowing pretty well what I would do to help him fulfill his vision. Kim gave me great material to work with, as he always did, and he was capable of the most important thing in this business - collaboration - getting help and both using and trusting in the talents of others. He is a great loss."

"My favorite Kim Manners memory was when you were filming in Big Bear," says Ilt Jones. "We were simulating the crash of a space ship in the middle of a forest, and it was supposed to be on fire. We had shut down two miles of road through the middle of the forest, about 30 miles from Big Bear, so we were a hundred or so miles from Los Angeles. It was about two o'clock in the morning and I was checking on the California Highway patrol officers who were at the barricades at both ends of the closed roads. I went up to one of them, and they said they were cold, so they went to get coffee for us. They drove off into the night, leaving me to sit on the hood of my car, under the night sky. All of a sudden this woman walks down the road towards me and asked if I was Ilt. My first response was, 'Oh my God. Who are you; why are you here, and how do you know my name?' She said she was a fan of the show and figured it was me since she heard my voice, saw I was tall, and had seen me on television. She said she was part of an Internet chat room of fans who had met in Los Angeles to come and see the filming. Then she points to an area full of trees and there were nine women huddled in darkness. I said, 'Thank you for coming out,' and before she walked away she asked me for an autograph. I was surprised at this since I don't do autographs; I'm just part of the back crew; I'm nobody. She told me that I was someone to her, and then proceeded to take out this concertina file and she pulls out this bundle of newspapers, magazines, and articles. And not just on me, but on David Duchovny, Gillian Anderson, and Kim Manners. After looking through the one inch thick pile of clippings, I signed it with,

'You guys are freaks. Love, Ilt.' She laughed; then went to show her friends, who all came up to me with the same concertina files full of these clippings, which I signed as well. After they left, I went back to the set and I told Kim about the girls. Kim said, in his usual joking manner, 'Jesus fucking Christ! Hunt those bitches down! Get the pictures back.' It was a classic Kim Manners moment, and we all started laughing about it."

"We have been very lucky to surround ourselves with feature Assistant Directors," Kim tells Matt Hurwitz. "Barry Thomas has done nothing but big features, and we brought him in here and we kind of hung that carrot in front of his face to direct one, which he did. And I've been working with Barry Thomas so long, but when it comes to numbers of extras and stuff, Barry knows. He knows what I want; and basically keep the set quiet when I'm trying to rehearse. He's a loyal guy. He decided he would stay with us through the end of this season, for that opportunity."

In addition to capturing the look associated with *The X-Files*, the cast and crew found ways to entertain themselves with on-set games made up by the crew.

"*Jimmy Happy Ball* was played by the cast and crew as we filmed for two weeks up in Big Bear. The game was named after a grip named Jimmy," Bill Roe tells me. "The orange ball was in a plastic water bottle, with a chain on it. At the beginning, the ball was passed around every hour to the next person on the list, which had about fifty names on it. Every hour the ball would change hands and you had to pass it off to the next person on the hour and you only had a minute do to so. The next person on the list had to be there to receive the ball. If you did not pass the ball off in a minute, you were penalized twenty dollars I think and it would go into the pot. After two weeks, it got down to every half hour, and then towards the end it was down to every ten or fifteen minutes. The winner of the game was the person left holding the ball when Kim called 'Wrap!' Kim would always have the same person next on the list, who I think was either a hair or make-up woman and he would literally jump into his van, drive to base camp, hand off the ball, and then come back and direct. It was hilarious. If the next person on the list was in the middle of a set up, we would place them in the van and bring them to Kim so he could pass off the ball. When Kim called wrap, I was the winner of the game. I won $850 cash from the pot so I walked over to Lake Arrowhead Inn where we're staying at and I asked the bartender how much the bar tab was. She replied that it was $750 so I gave her the $850. I think I had the money for about a half an hour."

Jimmy Happy Ball. Photo courtesy of Bill Roe.

I asked various cast and crew members about their time on the show, and if they had any favorite episodes or moments.

"There were a lot of moments, but I remember directing this little unit for *Squeeze* where Tooms inserts himself through a chimney," remembers Mat Beck. "No person can fit through the flute of a chimney, so we built a chimney set and a little bit of a rooftop on stage. We hired a contortionist and with a combination of mostly in camera effects and a little bit of roller scoping we could make it look like he was sitting inside a real chimney. That was a lot of fun. Another one is from *Jose Chung's From Outer Space* where we needed different kinds of aliens and one of them was a stop motion animation monsters. We put stunt coordinator Tony Morelli in a really cool suit and filmed him at a 120 frames per second, which is very slow motion, and then took out individual frames so it looks like the motion is really jerky. He walked towards us, reaches towards camera and grabs somebody and then a fight scene occurs. It was really fun because we were trying to make it look scary, funny, and slightly 'old school' and I thought it worked out well."

"Making stuff glow is not that hard in visual effects once you enter the land of the digital, you can put glowy stuff anywhere," continues Mat. "It's not that hard to do. Virtually anything I would do now, I would do at least slightly different than in the past. The tools of the trade are continually evolving, like the way you shoot elements, you might use motion control, costumes, miniatures, make-up and then there is a whole world of digital where you can synthesize pretty much anything. The mix between those techniques is shifting all the time, generally in favor of digital, but there are still ways to do them practically. For example, we experimented with various techniques and solutions for the black oil seen in the series and in the first movie. We would inject ink into water and some of the patterns we got were really beautiful so we used those and they worked great. Nowadays we could do that stuff purely digital, and you would get some really good effects, but the fun factor would be lost. You can name just about any effect, which we can do digitally, but setting up a camera at a pan of water with a syringe full of ink in it and having fun is cool. It is complex stuff, it's unpredictable, and it's more fun and serendipitous than trying to figure out all the variables before hand and pressing a button."

"On occasion, we would be doing a scene and we would get a call right before the scene because Chris would have re-written the scene," remembers actor Mitch Pileggi. "I remember one time David and I had a scene in a hospital and Chris called to say he had re-written a scene and he had to read it to us over the phone since the new sides had not been created yet. Of course, David has a photographic memory and I, on the other hand, have to struggle to remember my name. That was challenging for me since it was hard enough to memorize my lines as it was, but still a lot of fun."

"I remember we were in the pre-production meeting and we were discussing how the birds would perform on camera," recalls Ilt Jones on the episode *Chimera*. "Cliff Bole says, with a straight face, 'Don't worry, I'm looking forward to working with some professional crows.' He was not being funny, but we all busted out laughing because it was such a random, weird statement."

I asked Harry Bring, who is known for his comedic antics on location, what were some of the craziest thing he has done. "Probably walked into the set at 3am one morning, with my buck teeth and 'Coke Bottle' glasses and announced, at the top of my lungs that this was the worst freaking crew I had ever worked with. That became a standard line after that. I would actually be called in to set sometimes and pull some antics to liven up the joint because people were tired or it had gotten stale."

Harry Bring in character. Photo courtesy of Harry Bring.

Working on a fun location like the Santa Monica pier can be very tempting to pull practical jokes, especially with the multitude of extras on location. I asked the joker himself, producer Harry Bring, what his favorite gag was to pull on the unsuspecting public. "When we had group scenes, I would love to walk through the crowds with my whoopee cushion," laughs Harry. "The whole crew is just watching and waiting for me to rip one and get the reaction of the people around me."

While known for his creativity on *The X-Files*, some of the crew decided it was time to show Harry their version of a practical joke, with him as the unsuspecting target. "One night we shot some pickups on a Chris Carter directed show, which had a boat at a dock right behind my bungalow office. It may have been *Triangle*, but I'm not sure. I went home about midnight while they were still shooting because I had to be back in at 5am. When I came in the next morning, I found a 20 foot canoe inside my office. It was a practical joke pulled by our sound crew, headed by Steve Cantamessa. They had pulled the boat out of the water set and somehow got it in my office."

Practical jokes were not always needed to have a god time on or off camera. "The most fun I had on set would be when Krycek and I pushed CSM down the stairs and stepped over his believed to be dead body," recalls actress Laurie Holden. "I loved that day on the set; it was an exhilarating day and we made a little bit of television history. Nic is a fantastic actor and a super nice guy. I loved the scenes between Krycek and Marita because it was an opportunity to expose and explore this unbridled passion and heated emotion that had never been seen by these characters before. Our infamous love scene in *Patient X* was exciting because we both knew it would forever become a part of the show's lore. You know it's funny; film and television make everything look so much more glamorous than it ever actually is. And the amorous battleship embrace was no exception. We shot the scene multiple times from different angles and because of the nature of the movement, coming together in a rush of passion, well, we literally almost lost teeth. Every time our lips touched we were practically knocking each other's teeth out like two quarterbacks ramming together in a tackle. WHAM! My mouth hurt for a week! And Kim directed it with such style and integrity. It couldn't have been handled with more grace."

Composer Mark Snow has a unique viewpoint regarding some of the unique villains throughout the history of the series. "Sometimes there is a character, and it seems to come back a lot, where there is a real sympathy for, either the bad guy, the monster, or the dark character," continues Mark. "I always felt a melancholy sympathy for these characters and I always thought it really effective to show that in the music; that they were not all bad, but perhaps victims of circumstance or genetic engineering. I really felt empathy for a lot of these characters."

I asked Mark Snow if anyone, such as a director, influences him when he composes a score for the episodes. "Rob Bowman and I kind of got off to a shaky start because he wanted to throw his weight around some more than any of the other guys," recalls Mark. "I remember him hearing one of his episodes, and coming over and telling me his famous quote to me: 'what were you thinking when you wrote this!?' That can be taken both good and bad, but I think he meant it to be 'I thought it would be like this, not what you did'. From that point on we had such a great time together as I did with everyone, including Kim. With Rob, every time we would see each other we'd always open the conversation with 'What were you thinking?'"

"When Kim had the time to come to my studio and listen to the music for his shows, he would," continues Mark. "It wasn't every one that he did. It was always sort of a party mood at my place, whoever it was. I thought they were thrilled to be able to get out of the studio; I thought they were always excited to see what the music would do for the episodes that they slaved over. It never failed, that when Kim came over, he was like a kid in a candy store. When the music came on and he saw how the scenes would work with music, he just loved it. His reaction, all of a sudden, there was this new element to his work, that just enhanced and exaggerated in a good way what he had done already. I just don't remember him saying anything negative. I would just watch his face light. I wish he could have been there for all the shows."

"I felt that *The X-Files* was becoming something else from this entity that we were all a part of, that it had become different," shares David Duchovny. "I felt that *Hollywood A.D.* was about that. At the time of filming the end of *Hollywood A.D.*, Buena Vista Social Club was very popular and I had been listening to an instrumental cut on their first album, I don't remember what it was called, and I wanted to use it because I loved it. It felt happy to me and I wanted that sense of happiness for the dancing zombies at the end. Either we could not get the song or we could not afford it, so I asked Marked Snow, not to rip it off, but to give me a flavor like that. And that is exactly what he did; the piece came out really nice. In fact, Mark owes me big time because I sang his *X-Files* lyrics on the Rosie O'Donnell show and it made him happy. The lyrics were *The X-Files is a show with music by Mark Snow*."

In addition to Mark's musical genius, other crew members were able to contribute to the melodies on the shows. Producer Paul Rabwin tells me about his work on Season Seven.

"*Signs and Wonders* was a great show," recalls Paul Rabwin. "I was involved heavily with the music on that. Kim recognized the fact that I was really good with music and they needed a song for the snake handler scene because he's signing. I auditioned a bunch of gospel songs and spiritual songs for him and he asked me what I thought. I told him I could write one that was better and he told me to go for it. And I did. I wrote the spiritual song that they sing during the snake handler revival movement. Kim loved it. The name of the song is *May Glory Protect Us*. It was a great tribute that he was able to ask me and accept my opinion on it."

Producer Harry Bring comes from a musical family. I asked him if any of his parents Big Band talent rubbed off onto him. "I kick myself everyday when I think of this," replies Harry. "I didn't appreciate it at the time, but I do now. Music was initially crammed down our throats and all of us kids rebelled a little. I definitely did since I preferred to be outside playing little league than doing my piano scales. I played a little drums, a little piano, a little cello, but gave up on all of them after short periods of time. I now kick myself, wishing I could sit down and bang out a tune or score something. My father was a composer and arranger. Actually, the last episode we did on *Army Wives* was a flash back World War II episode. There were about five scenes in a USO club with a Glen Miller type band and they named it after my father's band, Lou Bring and his Orchestra. The woman who was singing portrayed my Mom. After she played with Benny Goodman and The Dorsey Brothers, she went to my dad's band and they fell in love."

Working with a close nit group for many hours a day leads to certain camaraderie among the crew. Barry Thomas, first assistant director, shared with me some of the gifts that were exchanged over the seasons.

"I can say that *The X-Files* was great for all sorts of swag," says Barry. "I've never worked on a show with so many generous departments. Every year most of the departments and many individuals gifted the entire crew with various sorts of memorabilia of their own creation: a fortune telling *X-Files* Eight Ball and David gave the entire crew autographed *Razor Scooters*. The Art Department did some wonderful thermal coffee mugs; the producers showered us with crew jackets, t-shirts, blankets, hats of every variety. Kim gave us all desert hats with a flap to protect or necks for a brutal shoot in the Borrego desert. We got water bottles, key chains, duffel bags. The Camera Department always had the coolest hats and bags. The grips and SFX departments did great T-shirts. Our co-producer Harry Bring spearheaded several annual events most famously annual golf tournaments attended by all of the regular cast members and most of the crew."

> **TOP 10-13 REASONS**
> **WE LOVE WORKING X-FILES:**
> THE HOURS ARE GREAT
> GET TO SEE THE SUNRISE AT LEAST ONCE A WEEK
> YA GOTTA LOVE THE SMOKE
> TINA'S WAFFLES
> TITO'S TACOS
> GLITTER FRIDAYS
> CANTAMESSA'S TV LOUNGE
> PARKING IS GREAT
> DON'T HAVE TO PLAN MANY WEEKENDS
> MEAL PENALITIES
> NEVER GET TO SEE PRIMETIME TELEVISION
> FREE T-SHIRTS
> BEST CREW AND COMPANY IN TOWN

Top 10-13 Reasons T-Shirt. Photo by Bill Roe.

"We also had bowling tournaments for the crew," continues Barry. "Chris Carter routinely rotated the gift of his killer season seats for the Los Angeles Dodgers, right in back of the catcher. The various vendors of the show contributed their company sponsored t-shirts and hats. Most of us were so swamped with swag that we didn't need to do Christmas shopping, we'd just re-gift from the stockpile we'd accrued over the course of each season."

> Hit it Steve, rolling!
> Bring in the thespians!
> Do they need to be painted?
> Bring in the worm!
> Bill Roe!
> Coffee Black.
> I guess nobody wants to go home tonight.
> Any movemnet yet? (usually asked after movement was just announced).
> Let's ask the gov.
> -Bucky ("I m Bucky")
>
> Why don't we all just step out?
> All right, we're ready, let's go.
> Very nice.
> I'm good, how you doin'?
> Don't wrap anything!
> -Bill Roe
>
> Bring me bam bam!
> HI! (in that highpitched squeal that can only be Tommy's voice.)
> If I had known, I would have...
> Yeah, we can do whatever you want, boss.
> -Tom Doherty
>
> Looks like we've done it again sir!
> Paula, this is Jono, how many more minutes do we have left?
> Righto!
> Will you be joining us on the balcony?
> What are the night shots?
> We're working here!
> -Jono
>
> Mitch, my bitch!
> Kim Manners remembers...
> Who do I have to blow...
> Elvis is up!
> -Carol Banker
>
> It's all about the hair.
> I need a drive by.
> -Dena Green
>
> Make up change? I'll need him in the trailer for at least 2 hours.
> -Cheri, facetiously of course
>
> "When are we moving?
> Are we going to lunch on time?
> What time is call tommorrow?
> Do I need a second meal?"
> -Tina
>
> "I Dunt feel so Good."
> -Hair and Make-up Dept. Motto

Figure 1. A page from *The X-Files Remembers* Sheet.

"Some of my favorite keepsakes I have kept over the years are slates that the crew has given me and a box full of T-Shirts that I have never opened," explains Bill Roe. "We started a thing in Season Six; I think Michael Watkins was responsible for this, where each department handed out T-Shirts every Christmas. So every year you received like ten T-Shirts, with everyone's name on the shirt, as well as some saying they were known for. I think there is a T-shirt full of Kim Mannerisms made by Barry Thomas, the first Assistant Director on a lot of Kim's episodes. I think it's called 'Mannerisms'', where one of his favorite sayings was 'Kick It In The Ass.' I think the 'Mannerisms'' T-Shirt had the most sayings."

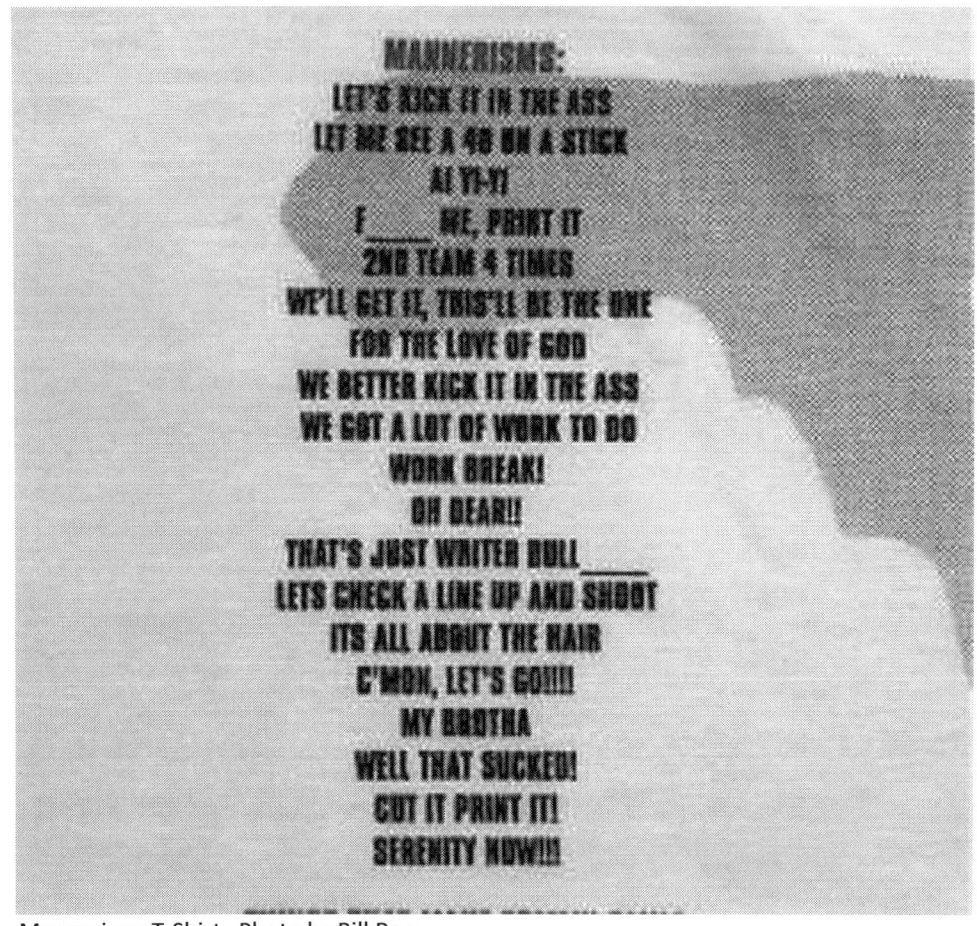

```
MANNERISMS:
LET'S KICK IT IN THE ASS
LET ME SEE A 40 ON A STICK
AI YI-YI
F____ ME, PRINT IT
2ND TEAM 4 TIMES
WE'LL GET IT, THIS'LL BE THE ONE
FOR THE LOVE OF GOD
WE BETTER KICK IT IN THE ASS
WE GOT A LOT OF WORK TO DO
WORK BREAK!
OH DEAR!!
THAT'S JUST WRITER BULL____
LETS CHECK A LINE UP AND SHOOT
ITS ALL ABOUT THE HAIR
C'MON, LET'S GO!!!!
MY BROTHA
WELL THAT SUCKED!
CUT IT PRINT IT!
SERENITY NOW!!!
```

Mannerisms T-Shirt. Photo by Bill Roe.

"I didn't keep any props from *The X-Files*, but I did keep my two-tone tango shoes from *The Lone Gunmen*," shares Bruce Harwood. "I do wish I'd managed to snag the T-shirt Kim had made up for one episode, the famous Double Salmon show, *Teso Dos Bichos*. It was two very beautiful images of pink salmon, one above the other. The climax is Mulder and Scully trapped underground with a bunch of house cats on the other side of the door. I did hear that one of the problems was that Gillian was allergic to cats, so someone had to make fake cats paws on sticks so they could film a cat attack on Scully, and everyone was laughing so hard during the filming that eventually Gillian just said 'that's it' and left the set. That show went through more script revisions than anyone on the crew had ever seen. Script revisions are printed in different colors; blue, pink, green, yellow, etc. This script went through the maximum color changes - twice. Kim had a T-shirt made for the crew that had a picture of two pink salmons on it."

In addition to crew T-shirts and Razor scooters, other souvenirs have made their way off set and into the personal collection of the cast and crew.

"One of my favorite souvenirs from the series is a plaster cast of David's face on my shelf in a reading area," shares Chris Carter. "It is a weird thing; the image is just so him, but it's a constant memory for me, of how much I owe David and Gillian for the success of the show. They were huge contributors to it."

"I kept the first Ramones shirt that I wore and a pair of glasses that I wore from the movie," shares Dean Haglund. "And of course, the chair back signed by everyone on the last day of shooting. David wrote, 'I am sorry we never had a sex scene.'"

"Some of the souvenirs I have from *The X-Files* are the bulldog that was sitting on top of Skinner's desk," says Mitch Pileggi. "I have it on top of my desk in the office at home. I look at it every day. I also had *The X-Files* pinball machine in my living room for the longest time until my wife finally said it had to go so we can get a dining room table. Now it's in storage."

Working on *The X-Files* was a dream come true to many people. For one, it was an opportunity to obtain his dream job.

"You know, Steven Spielberg called me to make a deal with me," Michael Watkins tells me. "I told him that I was loyal to the show, that I was under contract and I can't leave the show. The next thing I know, Chris called me and asks if I want to work for Steven Spielberg. I realized that Chris had made this call and was moving me and that's why I left the show. Working with Steven was something I had been pining for and been working on for years. Chris made my dream come true; he made a lot of my dreams come true. Chris was a unicorn in a time when there were none. He was the only one in the field that did it right. The measure of what he pulled off, whether it was idiosyncratic or creative, other people are trying to copy. And they can't do like Chris."

Naturally, there are usually some difficulties with a show like *The X-Files*. Time and budget are the usual culprits, but William B. Davis tells us lighting a cigarette was not always easy. "The most difficult thing to do on set or location was making sure the cigarette lighter lit," replies William when asked. "It seemed the more complicated the shot, the less likely it was to light."

"There were always wacky problems [in making an episode] and often those problems were time related," Mat Beck exclaims. "One of the big challenges and glories of T.V. is that you have to get it done quickly. There is a cliché: 'Nobody ever finishes a project, it's taken away from them.' That is very true of visual effects in post production. You have to get it done, it has to look good, and it has to look good by Thursday at two o'clock in the morning. Some of the most challenging things in the early days of *The X-Files* were literally delivering shows on the same day they would air, which you would never get away with doing now. I remember I was working on a show until Friday morning at six o'clock and it was going to be in your local living rooms that night. In fact, one of the measures of the hours you are working is when you are driving home from a session and you're listening to the early, live broadcast of Howard Stern on the radio, sleep for an hour or two, drive back into work and you're listening to the three hour delayed broadcast of Howard Stern. What really sucked about those hours is when you worked so late and you want to go home, it's no longer six o'clock in the morning, but quarter of eight in the morning and now you're into rush hour traffic trying to get home, with the sun in your eyes, trying not to fall asleep."

Season Seven Filming Locations

7x01 The Sixth Extinction

Written by: Chris Carter
Directed by: Kim Manners
Summary: Scully is in Africa trying to decipher the writings on the spacecraft. It contains passages from various religions and a map of our genetic makeup. At Mulder's request, Skinner brings in Michael Kritschgau to help him. There is abnormal activity in his brain making Mulder capable of remote viewing and mind reading. Scully returns to Washington to try and help Mulder, but after leaving Africa, the space craft appears to have disappeared.

Michael Kritsgau's Apartment
325 W. 3rd St.
Los Angeles, Ca

7x02 The Sixth Extinction: Amor Fati

Written by: Chris Carter & David Duchovny
Directed by: Michael Watkins
Summary: Mulder is in hospital, heavily sedated. Mulder has become an alien-human hybrid and immune to the alien virus. CSM wants to remove genetic material from Mulder's brain and transfer it to himself, and as Mulder is dreaming of a life of domestic bliss and creature comforts, the project doctors are operating on him. Scully finds Mulder still on the operating table after Diana Fowley has given her his location. Fowley is later killed.

Authors Note: Trying to pinpoint this location in Pacific Palasaides was an adventure. The house number that was given to me was not correct, so we drove up and down this affluent section near Malibu trying to recall the house, as one of my friends was pulling out my laptop and the episode. After about 15 minutes of trying to match the windows, and the driveway of the houses, we finally pinpointed #1146. As we finished taking our pictures of the location, the homeowners pulled in their driveway and stared at us. Their inquisitive stares were still seen in my rear view mirror until we turned the corner and drove off.

7x03 Hungry

Written by: Vince Gilligan
Directed by: Kim Manners
Summary: Rob Roberts, fast food restaurant employee, struggles with an eating disorder. He just can't get enough of those delicious human brains. After a fourth murder victim turns up with their brain missing, Mulder and Scully come to arrest him. Rob realizes he can't change who he is and charges at the agents, forcing Mulder to shoot him and end his life.

Hungry Boy Restaurant
McDonald's
4135 E. Firestone Blvd.
South Gate, Ca

Over Eater's Anonymous
1910 N. Commonwealth Ave.
Los Angeles, Ca

Rob's Apartment
1901 N. Commonwealth Ave.
Apartment #7
Los Angeles, Ca

"On the set of *Hungry*, we reconnected with Location Manager, Mac Gordon," share friends Adrienne Doucette and Joy Krone. "Having recently moved to California, we asked his advice on how to enter the industry. He was kind enough to connect us with a local production company, which launched our careers in this industry. We saw many things at this location for the first time. This is where we saw our first green screen effects shot when Rob transforms into his shark-like alter-ego. We were close enough to see them filming scenes with David Duchovny's photo double, Steve. We also witnessed the stunt when Rob's neighbor-turned-victim was disposed of into the garbage truck. This was an exciting episode of firsts for us in the production process"

On the set of *Hungry*. Photo by Adrienne Doucette.

In between takes on the set of *Hungry*. Photo by Adrienne Doucette.

7x04 Millennium

Written by: Vince Gilligan & Frank Spotnitz
Directed by: Thomas Wright
Summary: It is late December 1999. The bodies of four former FBI agents have been removed from their graves by a necromancer. They were all involved with the Millennium group so Mulder and Scully bring in former Millennium member Frank Black to help with the investigation. The necromancer is bringing the bodies back to life to prepare for the end of days they believe will come at the dawn of the new millennium. Mulder is trapped in a basement with the living dead, but Frank Black and Scully come to the rescue.

Hartwell Psychiatric Hospital
743 S. Lucerne Blvd.
Los Angeles, Ca

Mountain View Cemetery
2400 N. Fair Oaks Dr.
Altadena, CA
*** This site was also used in *Milagro*

"They were only filming interiors while we were on the set of *Millennium*, so we weren't able to see what was being filmed," say Joy Krone and Adrienne Doucette. "Nevertheless, we were excited to be there because we were huge fans of the series *Millennium* and were anxiously awaiting this crossover episode."

Crew sign for *Millennium*. Photo by Joy Krone.

7x05 Rush

Written by: David Amann
Directed by: Robert Lieberman
Summary: A sheriff's deputy is killed with super human force and Mulder and Scully are having doubts that the suspect Tony Reed, could have done it. They find that Tony and his friends, Max and Chastity, have discovered a cave which gives them super speed. When Max commits yet another murder, Tony and Chastity want to turn him in. They try to get to the cave before Max, but he's already there. With a single shot Chastity manages to kill both Max and herself, leaving Tony alone in a slow-moving world.

High School
William McKinley Elementary
325 S. Oak Knoll Ave.
Pasadena, Ca

"We had the amazing experience of playing high school students in this episode," Adrienne Doucette and Joy Krone share with me. "This was our first time as background extras on the show, as opposed to being passive observers. We were in the classroom scene taking the test, in the cafeteria, and in the hallway. The crew knew us from our previous set visits and made us feel right at home. During the filming of the cafeteria scene, we were directed to hide behind the Coke machine for the part when a table crushes the teacher. One of David's stunt doubles, Brett, played a trick on us during the scene. He came up and shook the machine and scared us to make us laugh. He was a fun guy and the crew was very cool to us. The experience was just amazing on *Rush*; easily the best experience we've had as extras."

7x06 The Goldberg Variation

Written by: Jeffrey Bell
Directed by: Thomas Wright
Summary: Henry Weems is the luckiest man in the world. When he plays poker with the mob, he wins. When they suspect him of cheating and throw him off a skyscraper, he survives. He needs money to pay for the treatment of a terminally ill boy in his building. When the mob finds out that Weems has agreed to testify against them they kidnap the boy's mother to try and get at him. However, in an amazing sequence of events, the mobsters end up dead and one of them turns out to be a perfect donor match for the little boy.

Jimmy Catrona's Apartment
537 Spring St.
Los Angeles, Ca

Floor Elevator
544 S. Grand Ave.
Los Angeles, Ca

Henry Williams & Maggie and Ritchie LaPone's Apartment Building
451 S. Bixel St.
Los Angeles, Ca

Lotto Market
Chicago Meat Market
735 S. Chicago St.
Los Angeles, Ca

"*The Goldberg Variation* was the first time I was able to see Gillian and David work together, and I learned exactly how hard it is to truly lock down a set when you are on location," fan Patricia Steffy informs me. "At two different points, production was stopped because random people realized that they had happened upon the location shoot. The first time involved a teenager. She was across the street and apparently just realized what was going on-- at which point she started yelling David Duchovny's name and dancing. All this climaxed with a rather impressive twirl around a street lamp ala *Singing in the Rain*. David was amused enough to stand up and applaud while getting the rest of the cast and crew to join in. I thought they were going to have to redo Gillian's make-up she was laughing so hard."

"The second time production stopped had to do with another woman passing by the set," continues Patricia. "We were all in place to start shooting the scene from a new angle. The director was about to get things rolling, and all of a sudden we heard this woman yell out, "Oh My God'. Apparently, as she was stuck in traffic at a red light, she realized what was happening around her. She kept looking up at the light and then back at us and screaming, 'Oh My God'. We all just stopped and started laughing. It was so sudden, and then we couldn't do anything else until traffic moved, and she stopped screaming. I don't blame her, if it had been me, I might have been tempted to do the exact same thing."

The *Goldberg Variations* Mini Mart. Photo by Adrienne Doucette.

"Mac Gordon cautioned us to only visit this location during the daytime," warns Joy Krone and Adrienne Doucette about the mini market scene. "We were young girls, and he was concerned for our safety. Fortunately, there was plenty of action during the day. The day we were there, we saw the stunt where Henry Weems, lottery ticket in hand, is run over by a truck in the middle of the road."

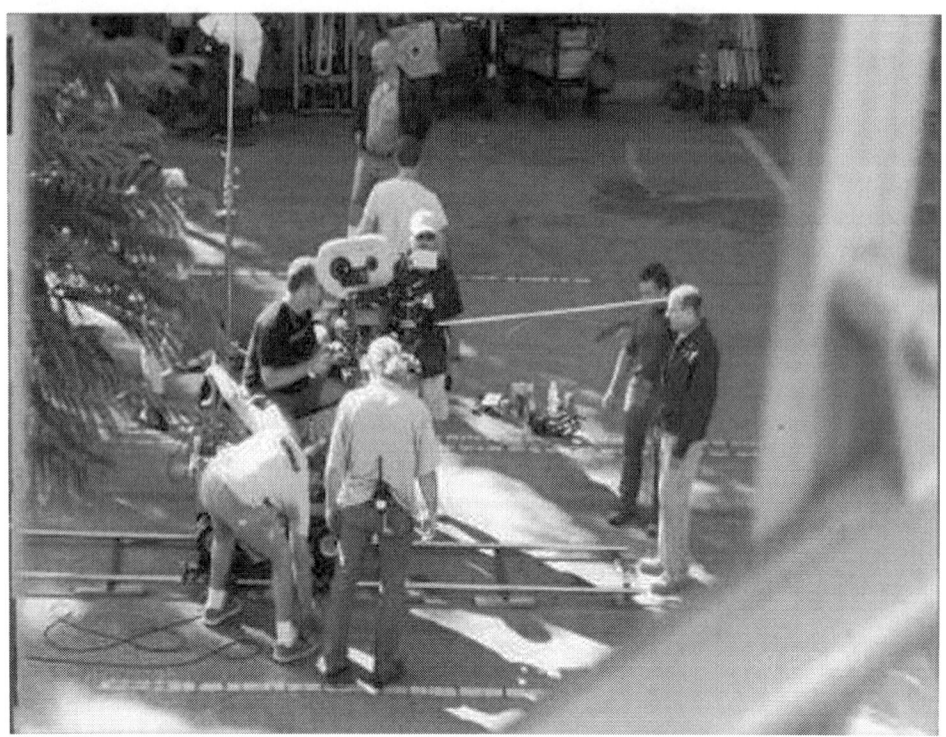

On the set of *Goldberg Variations*. Photo by Adrienne Doucette.

7x07 Orison

Written by: Chip Johannessen
Directed by: Rob Bowman
Summary: Donnie Pfaster, a death fetishist put behind bars by Mulder and Scully back in season 2, escapes from prison. He is helped by Reverend Orison who let prisoners out so that he can pass judgment on them himself. Pfaster kills the reverend and goes after Scully, the one who got away. He hides in her apartment and attacks her, but she manages to free herself and eventually kills him.

Bus Stop/Diner
7447 Firestone Blvd.
Downey, Ca

7x08 The Amazing Maleeni

Written by: Vince Gilligan, John Shiban, & Frank Spotnitz
Directed by: Thomas Wright
Summary: Magician the Amazing Maleeni performs a trick where he turns his head completely around. When he is discovered dead in his truck, his head falls off. Scully's autopsy reveals that the man died of heart disease over a month ago and his head was merely glued onto the body. The agents unravel a plan scheme set in motion by Maleeni's twin brother and his magician friend, LaBonge, to not only frame an excellmate of LaBonge, but also to get away with a whole lot of money through electronic funds transfers.

Santa Monica Pier
100 Santa Monica Pier
Santa Monica, Ca

Pool Hall
North Hollywood Billiards
11128 Magnolia Blvd.
North Hollywood, Ca

Magic Theater
NoHo Arts Theater
11136 Magnolia Bld.
North Hollywood, Ca

First Private Bank and Trust
Cradock Maine Bank
520 Broadway Ave.
Santa Monica, Ca

Authors Note: My friend and I actually did not have an exact address for the Craddock Maine bank in this episode. We ended up in

Santa Monica, wandering the busy streets, looking for anything familiar. Since I was driving an SUV, we were able to use all the windows, in addition to the moon roof. Suddenly, in the near distance, we saw the black windows of 13 story diamond tipped bank. While navigating traffic, my navigator verbally gave me instructions and we ended up parked in almost the exact spot where the shot was captured for the episode.

7x09 Signs & Wonders

Written by: Jeffrey Bell
Directed by: Kim Manners
Summary: When a young man is found killed by no less than 116 snake bites, our agents are led to the Church of Signs and Wonders. The young man and his pregnant girlfriend, Gracie, recently left the church which practiced snake handling and a very strict interpretation of the Bible. The church's Reverend O'Connor, and Gracie's father, is suspected of murdering the man, but it turns out that it is Reverend Mackey of the community church who is behind not only the murder, but also Gracie's pregnancy. Gracie gives birth to snakes and her father goes to confront Mackey. Mulder intervenes, but is attacked by snakes. Reverend Mackey disappears.

Jarred Chirp Residence
Melody Ranch Motion Picture Studio
24715 Oak Creek Ave.
Newhall, Ca

Church of God: Signs and Wonders
Melody Ranch Motion Picture Studio
24715 Oak Creek Ave.
Newhall, Ca

Blessing Church
Piru Church
3875 Center St.
Piru, Ca
***Note: This church is located literally down the street from the house used in *How the Ghosts Stole Christmas.*

The Blessing Church from *Signs and Wonders*. Photo by Erica Fraga.

7x10 Sein Und Zeit

Written by: Chris Carter & Frank Spotnitz
Directed by: Michael Watkins
Summary: Mulder requests the case of a young girl who disappears from her bed. A note left behind makes a reference to Santa Claus. Mulder's mother hears of the case and tries to get hold of him before committing suicide. Mulder thinks the kidnapping case is connected with

his sister's disappearance. By chance they come across Santa's North Pole Village and find the kidnapper - and the graves of many children.

La Cresenta Motel
2413 Foothill Blvd.
Glendale, Ca
***This site was also used in *This Is Not Happening* and *The Truth II*

This episode may or may not have landed one crew member in jail according to one Season 7 crew member. "A props assistant was out picking up props from various places, one of which was the ransom note from *Sein Und Zeit* 7x10 or *Closure* 7x11. He went to use a payphone and for some reason had the note in his pocket. He took it out when searching for quarters and set it down in the booth, and then he left the note behind on accident. Well, the next person who went to use the pay phone sees the note and calls the police. When the assistant returned for the note, the police were waiting to take him away."

7x11 Closure

Written by: Chris Carter & Frank Spotnitz
Directed by: Kim Manners
Summary: Mulder is approached by Harold Piller, a police psychic, who claims to have information about the kidnapping case. He says the girl, and other children like her, have been taken by walk-ins. Piller receives a message from Mulder's mother which leads them to a deserted military base. Here Mulder finally learns what happened to his sister all those years ago.

Motel
Best Western Motel
Mulder's Room #121
5525 Sepulveda Blvd.
Sherman Oaks, Ca

Denny's Restaurant
5525 Sepulveda Blvd.
Sherman Oaks, Ca

Closure finally allowed Mulder to solve the mystery regarding his sister's whereabouts. According to many fans, the night scene in the woods is one of the most cinematically powerful shots in the entire series. Matt Allair, creator of *The X-Files Lexicon*, was kind enough to share the following interview done with Director Kim Manners from his website concerning the powerful reunion scene at the end of this episode.

"It was an opportunity for a director to take a beautifully written word and just a beautiful emotional content and run with it, you know," says Kim. "That dolly shot across the kids playing in the foreground as Mulder comes up the hill and he appears and he comes between the kids, and it. The wonder of him looking at those children and them staring up at him; and the little girl that he stopped and looked down to; she looked up at him and then he turns and looks past camera. The look on his face was just so peaceful."

"We cut to his sister running up," continues Kim. "In the script, it called for his sister to run up and hug him and Mulder was to start crying. David didn't want to cry. He said, 'No, I just don't think that's the right choice.' I said, 'David, you know, this is your sister. You know, you're finally realizing, whether it's subconscious or not, that your sister is in fact dead. We've come a long way to get to this answer, and I think it's a very emotional time for Mulder.' He said, 'Just watch what I do, just trust me.' And he held that little girl actress. There was a beatific smile on his face that was absolutely astounding. I printed it and I said to him after the sequence was shot, I said, 'You were absolutely right, and I learned something here today.' You know, it was a beautiful sequence, it really was."

"I don't really recall approaching Kim and suggesting that Mulder look at peace when he finds Samantha, but it sounds like me and it sounds like Kim," remembers David Duchovny when I share Kim's interview. "What happens after a year or two on series television is the actors become the custodian of the characters; directors, even someone like Kim who had directed 53 episodes for *The X-Files*, they come and they go. The actors at some point are really making the big choices. Regarding the scene with Mulder and Samantha's spirit, it's something I might run by Chris or Kim, but it would have been an instinctual thing that would have happened on set. Kim was always great with that. He was an enthusiast and if he saw that you were enthusiastic about something, he would trust that."

Mark Snow recalls the moving pieces composed for the episode, and for the reunion scene in particular. "I suppose it was a sense of biblical fervor and religiosity - an elegy - a feeling about it that was so poignant and touching to me," says Mark. "There was something very moving about it, where I could use my experiences as a student at Julliard, with my love for early Renaissance music."

"Things were so amazing to me," continues Mark. "It seems like a perfect fit; me and this show. I was so inspired by it, turned on by it, and the best thing was I felt this fantastic freedom to try anything I wanted. When we started off with the pilot, they had taken a lot of music from other scores and they said we like this, we like that, do it this way, do it that way. And I did at the beginning. Those things were mainly atmospheric, sound design, and then it became more musical and I just started creeping things in slowly and surely and they didn't say anything. Just keep going, however you feel it. That was one of the best things. Out of all the shows, *The X-Files* was exceptional. I would always laugh when they would call me up and say this is the worst one yet; we need your help. So I'm bracing for something hideous and the thing shows up and it's terrific."

"In *Closure*, we were extras at the diner," Joy Krone and Adrienne Doucette share with me. "We were walking outside the scene where Mulder and Scully were sitting at the table with Harold Pillar. When the night scene in the diner came up, we hoped we could have the opportunity to stay. Assistant Director Nina Jack approached Kim Manners and asked if we could be used in the scene. Kim said that we looked way too young to be in this diner late at night, so he couldn't use us. However, to our great delight and appreciation, he allowed us to stick around even though we weren't used in the night scene."

7x12 X-Cops

Written by: Vince Gilligan
Directed by: Michael Watkins
Summary: It's a full moon and Mulder and Scully are in Los Angeles looking for a werewolf when they suddenly find themselves in the middle of an episode of *COPS*. They now have to deal with a camera crew tagging along wherever they go, much to Mulder's delight and Scully's annoyance. As more and more victims turn up they realize they're not looking for a werewolf after all, but rather a creature that feeds on mortal fear and will take the shape of your worst nightmare.

Mini Mart where Ricky shot
Venice Ranch Market
425 Rose Ave.
Los Angeles, Ca

The refurbished crack house from *X-Cops*. Photo by Erica Fraga.

Author's Note: In confirming the location for the Crack House used in *X-Cops*, my companions and I were surprised to find the home totally refurbished, and replaced as a duplex. I even contacted Ilt Jones and Mac Gordon to confirm the address. The residence on Flower Ave looks nothing like the house used in the episode.

"*X-Cops* (7x12) was a good show for me to do," states director Michael Watkins. "I am an ASG cameraman and that was such a visual show that it was really easy for me to put it in my mind. It was really just a matter of extending the borders of the shooting lines. For example, if you pull up to an intersection, I made two intersections out of it. I had helicopters flying up and down Venice and things like that. It was a lot of fun for me and I really enjoyed it. I was able to do an enormous amount of page count – 12 pages in 8 hours - in one set up. We spent a lot of time rehearsing, talking about who was where and then just take off with the handheld camera. David really liked that, embraced it and got right behind that. The big thing with this episode was the police car that flipped over. We strapped ourselves into it with the camera so everything was spinning and turning. It was completely safe and looked pretty good."

"*X-Cops* was the hardest episode for us," recalls Mac Gordon. "It was a brutal episode for me and my team because we were out all night, on foot, with cameras and stuff running around Venice. We were everywhere. We had helicopters come in low, we had gun fire, we had a car wreck; we had amazing amounts of stuff. It took us a long time to prep all that stuff and it's a tough part of town to work on since lots of movie people are there. And movie people are the worst; it can be a hindrance to what you need to do. My partner, Ilt Jones, scouted this house that was supposed to be this crack house. He went for the authentic thing and it turned out it was a real crack house. We wound up having to move the family out – and their seven pit bulls. They caused a ruckus at the first motel so we had to move them to a second motel. The house was amazing. There were people dealing drugs while my construction guys were trying to fix up the front porch. It was an experience."

7x13 First Person Shooter

Written by: William Gibson & Tom Maddox
Directed by: Chris Carter
Summary: The Lone Gunmen call in Mulder and Scully when a man is killed inside a virtual reality video game. The killer is a female character which no one programmed into the game. When another player turns up dead Mulder goes into the game to kill her, but he disappears inside the game. Scully goes after him and takes on the rogue character.

Enterprise-Rent-A-Car
Alfred Mann Foundation
First Person Shooter
25134 Rye Canyon Loop
Santa Clarita, Ca

Western Town
Melody Ranch Motion Picture Studio
24715 Oak Creek Ave.
Newhall, Ca

"I have a very creative gaffer named Jono Kouzouyan and he has done a lot of features and we have known each other a long time," Bill Roe tells me. "We had a fantastic time coming up with ideas in the spur of the moment on *The X-Files*. It was just a white building when we showed up there that day to film *First Person Shooter*. We came up with this idea of putting lights partway up the walls, and putting white, fluorescent kelflows on the floor just to break up the floor; to have something else. We always try and make an' X' somewhere in the episodes. At the end of the episode, there are these two beam lights in the background that make an X. It's a fun thing to do and we did it throughout the series. Not too many people saw this, but I did hear on websites that people would say stuff like, "I saw five X's today in this episode. We did try and stay away from top light on *The X-Files*. We never liked top light. It's not very flattering and I don't particularly like it. There were instances that we did use it, but in a scene where someone is talking it's better to put the light on the floor than on the ceiling."

According to Chris Carter, Kim Manners was very helpful when he filmed this episode. "I would watch Kim in scenes where he would go in, particularly on set, and that helped me on *First Person Shooter* 7x13," Chris tells me. "It was a really hard episode and it was hard to do the work in the time allotted. I had a scene, where I tried to do a oner myself, and it just didn't work. A oner was not a hard and fast rule, but it was really to protect ourselves editorially. A oner is a shot that has no cut in it; it is a long take. And they are murder dramatically if the dramatic tension flags at all or if there is any mistake or hiccup in the camera move or performances. If done well and stylishly, they can be amazing. You see them all the time in movies, like in a Robert Zemeckis film. In short, it is a shot that encompasses the whole scene in one take. It didn't work because I did not do something I had seen Kim do when he re-shot that scene for me. I watched him go in and tear out walls and other obstacles for a camera position. Kim was not afraid to dig in and make it work. He knew what he was capable of in the time given to him and how to push the limits."

"Also in First *Person Shooter*," continues Chris, "I had a shot, which was a stylish little action piece where the female avatar goes to kick David in the face, and he catches her high heel in front of his face," remembers Chris. "I staged it kind of interestingly and it turned out pretty and I remember Kim saying to me, 'Cool!' I think that everyone was so competitive on the show; I think Kim was the star. Rob Bowman was there first and he the star, but when Rob left Kim rose to the top and that is where I think he considered himself to be as a director. I would have to agree that Kim was the leader of a group of people that did particular, good work."

"Working with Kim and Rob on their episodes was interesting; they have a diametric way of dealing with us location managers," says Ilt Jones. "Kim Manners would tell us to have fun with the scouting – pretend you're the director. Rob Bowman would say something like, 'So, you want to be the director?' I was trying to think creatively about what was required. For example, the script would call for an apartment block with a three story stucco based, beige valley apartment block and all of my creative sensibilities would rebel against that. So I would bring them what was called for, but then I would show them something else much more interesting and Kim would love it. When this script came out for *First Person Shooter*, the script called for a housing project area, but needed to have gun battles and roaring motorcycles at night. I told Chris that we could find such a place, but that it would be very expensive and very restricted since the action is at night. Kim's words gave me the courage to offer up another suggestion for the episode; a place called Wyckoff building in the warehouse district in downtown Los Angeles, near 7th and Alameda. It has wonderful alley ways and great fire escapes and great geometry. I said this would be a great place to shoot it since it has a digitized feel to it; it looked like it could be in a video game. They loved the fact that I brought the location to the table, which was more interesting and worked really well for the episode. In fact, I have a signed *First Person Shooter* poster from the episode, personalized by Chris, David, and Gillian, hanging in my home office. It reminds me of the confidence I had to put that second option forward as an alternative. It was a direct result of Kim's enthusiasm and encouragement."

First Person Shooter poster. Photo by Ilt Jones.

"Kim Manners encouraged me to think outside the box, and it has had a profound influence on my career ever since and I am forever, eternally grateful," affectionately says Ilt.

7x15 En Ami

Written by: William B. Davis
Directed by: Rob Bowman
Summary: The Cigarette Smoking Man claims to be dying and says he wants to do something good before he dies. He convinces Scully to go with him to meet a contact, Cobra, from the Department of Defense who has been working on technology that can cure any disease. He's worried that it will fall into the wrong hands and wants Scully to have it. CSM gives her the disc, however, the disc turns out to be empty.

Gas Station
29983 Mulholland Hwy.
Agoura Hills, Ca

Saddle Creek Restaurant
419 Cold Canyon Rd.
Calabasas, Ca

Like most projects, shows produced on *The X-Files* undergo an editing process before they reach the air. Writer and actor, William B. Davis, related the story of his directorial episode *En Ami* (7x15). An avid water skier himself, I had to know if William ever saw Cancer Man on a lake.

"In an early draft, we had Cigarette Smoking Man waterskiing, teaching Scully how to water ski, but it was all a little fanciful," chuckles William. "When Chris Carter found out that I was a water-skier, he wanted to do an episode with Smoking Man waterskiing, but that never happened. One day I asked him about that; he told me that the other writers talked about it and did not find it totally convincing. That's the one thing I would have liked to have gone into that episode, but didn't. Kim and I also talked about water skiing a lot, because he was a water skier. We shared notes on what kind of slalom ski we used and what kind of boats we skied behind, but we never did get a chance to ski together. I did talk about it more with Rob Bowman, who was a more serious water skier."

William B. Davis in action.
Photo courtesy of William B. Davis.

"I know when we were shooting [this episode] there was a complicated water scene, in which we had cameras on the water and we had things coming in from the lake," continues William. "It really needed another director to really monitor that. The only director that Rob would trust to do that extra days work, as a co-director, was Kim."

"Joy and I were extras in the beginning scene, where people were protesting the decision of the parents to not treat their son's cancer," Adrienne Doucette tells me. "We had to bang on the car and hold up signs. We were out in the rain for hours and the red paint from my sign dripped all over my suede jacket. After six hours, I was cold and miserable and practically in tears. The PA offered to cover the cost of replacing my jacket (with production money), which had been ruined by the red paint. This was an exceptionally generous offer, especially considering the rain was not an artistic choice of a television show, but an act of Mother Nature."

7x17 all things

Written by: Gillian Anderson
Directed by: Gillian Anderson
Summary: Scully discovers that an ex-boyfriend and medical school teacher, Daniel Waterston, is in the hospital with a heart condition. Through a vision, Scully sees that Daniel is sicker than his doctors think and with the help of one of Mulder's contacts, they try an alternative approach to get him well. Daniel survives and wants to get back together with Scully, but she turns him down, realizing she is not the same person anymore.

FOX lot
10201 Pico Blvd.
Los Angeles, Ca

Chinatown
900-977 N. Broadway Ave.
Los Angeles, Ca

Waterson's Hospital
John Ferraro Building
111 N. Hope St.
Los Angeles, Ca

Kim Manners was a guiding hand to Gillian in her directorial debut. "When Gillian was directing *all things* (7x17), she went to Chris and said *I want to write and I want to direct this*," Kim told Matt Hurwitz in 2002. "*But I want Kim on the set with me to kind of help me through it.* So they kind of arranged the schedule so that I was available. I went over Gillian's homework with her almost every day. And Gillian had a tough time with crossing the line, when who looks right to left, who looks left to right. And she had some shots that – they haven't invented that lens yet. There were some camera moves she wanted to do, and I saw, you can certainly do that, but what are you going to do after lunch, you know? I mean, you've got to keep in mind your schedule here. So I found ways to help her compromise and still get kind of what she wanted."

"Long story short, I was with her every step of the way and made sure that her picture was going to cut, and she did a terrific job," continues Kim to Matt. "She probably directed 70-75% of it on her own, and I tweaked it for 25 to 30%. Well, the show aired about a month later and the fans got on the Internet, they loved the show. So a month later I had an episode on that I had directed, and one of the fans got on the Internet and said how nice it was to see that Gillian Anderson's directing style had rubbed off on Kim Manners. I thought, well gee, thanks a lot. I've only been doing this for 23 years, or whatever it was, and finally I've got somebody – she was embarrassed. She was truly embarrassed."

"The producers were telling me this was not going to be an easy episode," discloses Mark Snow about *all things*. "They told me when she comes over to listen to the music, she will have a lot of notes and I should prepare myself. So she came in, and she brought her own lunch – some kind of salad – and we go into the studio and she sits on the floor and opens up her salad and starts munching on it and says, 'Okay, Let's hear it.' So we play it and she just loved it. I saw her going into sort of mini contortions, trying to think of something to say. 'How about...', 'Make it....', 'No, no, it's just right.' There really were very little notes, if any, that I got from her. I think she was pleasantly surprised because it was a different sound. I chose a certain style that was new agey, minimal since I had a little advance warning that she was not looking for the standard X-Files music sound, but something off the beaten track. I was alerted in time and I think it worked out great. It was a pretty pleasant experience."

"When I was on the set of *all things*, we were filming in and around Chinatown," says Joy Krone. "I was close to video village, the place where all the monitors and Director and Producer chairs are. Kim Manners was on set, helping Gillian since it was her directorial debut. Gillian would ask him questions and he would give her feedback and guide her along. Throughout the day, Kim kept glancing back at me as if I looked really familiar to him. Then his eye caught mine, so I waved and said hi. He asked me, 'Are you John Bartley's daughter?' John Bartley was the Director of Photography for the first three seasons in Vancouver. I told him no, but that I met John Bartley on the set of another television show and saw him on occasion. Then Kim told me, 'Wow. You look exactly like his daughter.' And that was the extent of my conversation with Kim. After that, I enjoyed observing from the closeness of video village even though I wasn't in the scenes being filmed."

"I shot the episode *all things* on February 28, 2000," remembers Patricia Steffy. "While I had shot episodes of *The X-Files* before this, they had all been location shoots. My day on *all things* was my first time shooting on the lot. At this point, I knew a couple of crew members, and one in particular I never saw outside of *The X-Files* because of their crazy shooting schedule. So being on the lot gave me a chance to not only see Gillian Anderson direct David Duchovny, but also hang out with my friend."

"When we finished shooting in the morning, my friend asked me if I'd like to see the standing sets," continues Patricia. "Of course, I jumped at this chance! We walked around the FBI. I gazed at Mulder's office and then headed over to Mulder's apartment which they were dressing for the shooting that afternoon. I'm not sure if it was my imagination or not, but there seemed to be an awful lot of very entertaining and 'adult' sounding literature as set dressing. After taking a few minutes to appreciate 'the couch', we headed into Mulder's bedroom, which was also being dressed for the afternoon's shoot."

"As you can tell from the scenes, there was a ton of stuff in his bedroom," recalls Patricia. "Naturally, in order to take it all in, I had to sit on Mulder's bed. Do you have any idea how difficult it is to maintain a professional demeanor when you are hanging out on Mulder's bed? It was then that I noticed what looked like a brandy snifter full of condoms on his bedside table. My observation prompted the question, 'What does Mulder need condoms for? He never gets any.' All of a sudden, my friend wouldn't say anything and started avoiding conversation about the episode —which, of course, made me instantly suspicious. About 20 minutes later, I was reading the sides and realized why he refused to say anything."

TEASER

BLACKNESS

We hear the faint sound of WATER DRIPPING. One solitary drop at a time. The water echoes quietly as we:

CUT TO:

2) CLOSE - SCULLY'S FACE

What little light there is seems to dance and sway from above. She looks straight at us, with an ever-so-slight, peaceful smile. Slowly, we ADJUST TO REVEAL we're:

INT. BATHROOM - NIGHT

Scully is looking at a reflection of herself in the mirror. The swaying light reflected from a single bare bulb attached to a ceiling fan, rotating lazily.

Scully buttons her shirt, straightens her skirt. She's dressing.

SCULLY
Ten.

Finished, Scully moves past us, exiting frame. HOLD ON the empty bathroom, CAMERA FINDING the dripping faucet.

3) INT. ANOTHER ROOM - NIGHT

Moonlight, broken by a tangle of branches pressing against a window. Scully bends to pick up her jacket. She shrugs into it, and we move in CLOSER. Her eyes are fixed on something o.s. We HOLD ON her there for just a beat, before she leaves frame.

As she does, CAMERA DRIFTS across the room to a BED. Finding a naked thigh in a mass of crumpled blankets, then a BARE ARM... finally settling on a FACE: MULDER. Asleep. HOLD on this image, as we hear a door close in the b.g. The solitary drip, drip, drip, and we hear a CACHUNK, as we:

CUT TO BLACK:

END OF TEASER

Call sheet from *all things*. Image provided by Patricia Steffy.

7x18 Brand X

Written by: Steve Maeda & Greg Walker
Directed by: Kim Manners
Summary: A Morley tobacco company whistle blower dies under mysterious circumstances the night before he's going to give testimony before a federal grand jury. Morley has been genetically altering the tobacco plants to produce a safer cigarette, but that has created genetically altered tobacco beetles as well. Their eggs are transported into the lungs through tobacco smoke where they grow into beetles, killing the person who inhaled the smoke as they exit the body.

Morley Headquarters
Union Station
700 N. Alameda St.
Los Angeles, Ca

"*Brand X* and *Fight Club* were overlapping each other," shares Kathleen Keegan. "For a couple of days we were out in Pasadena watching them film on Locksley Dr. Everyone was really nice to us again, telling us where to stand so we were out of the way and so we get to see everything. There was not a lot of filming going on outside, but we were told the reason this house was chosen was because the actual owners of the house had this awesome art collection inside and they thought it looked really good to play as this doctor's house. When you see the episode, you can see the amount of art they had inside. Plus the episode took place in Winston-Salem, North Carolina and they thought the house looked 'East Coast' with the cedar shingles. We did see them film Mulder and Scully arriving to the house after the death had occurred, so we got to see a little outside action."

"Earlier in the day, Gillian had come over to sign autographs for us and I had never received her autograph before," recalls Kathleen. "I had this metallic silver liquid pen that you have to shake to get it to work. She shook the pen and when she went to take the cap off, the ink splattered all over the place. She had this beautiful Donna Karen suit and navy blue trench coat on and we both jumped back away from each other and screamed. I asked her if she was okay, to which she replied, 'I don't care about me. Did you get any on you?' I told her, 'Me? I'm not the one wearing a $5,000 Donna Karen suit!' She said not to worry about that since there were five more sitting on the rack!"

"At one point, when they broke for lunch, we walked to a nearby McDonald's around the corner and down the street," recollects Kathleen. "As we were coming back up the street with our food, we see Mitch sitting on the corner, eating a sandwich. We were on the other side of the street so as not to interrupt his lunch and we walk by to which he says, 'Hi! How ya doing?' and strikes up a conversation with us. He asks us what we got for lunch and we offered to go back and get him something when he said he was just going to eat his peanut butter and jelly sandwich. Before we left him to his lunch, we tried again to offer him a sandwich, but he declined. Before we left, Mitch offered to sign some stuff if we had any. He went to sign my stuff and I had the same metallic silver pen with me. Before I gave it to him I told him I would take the cap off for him and told him what happened to Gillian. Mitch then tells me jokingly, 'Oh, she's such a mess.'"

"What really made this location interesting was watching the cast hang out outside," continues Kathleen. "David and Mitch were goofing off in the front of the house, which has this huge front lawn and chestnut trees since it's set back from the street. The front lawn was covered with the round, prickly pods from the trees that contain the chestnut. The men were throwing them at each other and then they decided to play baseball with them. David started to pitch the pods at Mitch, as he tried to hit them with a stick from the lawn. Mitch missed every single one. Then they switched and Mitch pitched the pods to David. David hit every single pitch and you heard the 'crack' of the connection. David went back inside for something, which leaves Mitch to amuse himself with the pods.

He throws them up into the air and then catches it. One of them hit him on the head and makes his head bleed. He had to call over make-up to touch up his head. Later on he comes over to us and asks if we saw that 'bone head' move of his. We told him we didn't want to say anything, but yeah, we saw and heard it and we asked him if he was okay. He smiled and said just his pride was bruised."

"For the night shoot, we were at the second doctor's house, Dr. Voss, in Encino," says Kathleen. "This was the first time I had ever met and spoken to Ilt Jones, the location manager. He was so nice and so funny. We were talking to Mitch, and then Ilt came over to tell us how he appreciates us coming out and showing support for the show and then says, 'Isn't this boring? Isn't it like watching paint dry?' We began to ask questions about the shoot and what was going to happen and he flat out told us where they were going to be filming the next day, and that David was going to be there, and starts spouting off all this information. When he's done he looks over at us and says, 'Why am I telling you all this? I shouldn't be telling you this at all.' We told him we didn't mind, but we appreciated it."

7x19 Hollywood A.D.

Written by: David Duchovny
Directed by: David Duchovny
Summary: Skinner is helping out a writer/producer friend from Hollywood who is doing research for a movie and lets him tag along with Mulder and Scully on a case. They're investigating a bombing in a church where they also find forgeries of a fake gospel as well as the body of the man who made them, Micah Hoffman. They suspect that Cardinal O'Fallen at the church is behind the bombing after they discover Hoffman has been blackmailing him. As they go to make the arrest, Hoffman walks in very much alive. Mulder and Scully are suspended and go to California to watch the movie loosely based on them being made.

Lazarus Bowl movie theater
FOX lot
Daryl Zanuck Theater
10201 Pico Blvd.
Los Angeles, Ca

Church from Teaser
St. Andrew's Catholic Church
311 N. Raymond Ave.
Pasadena, Ca

Diner
Shakers
601 Fair Oaks Ave.
South Pasadena, Ca

Crew sign for *Hollywood A.D.*. Photo by Joy Krone.

"I thought seeing Skinner with that young girl was really a stretch; I really didn't think much of that," recalls Mitch Pileggi of his time on *Hollywood A.D.* "I thought it was inappropriate for the character. I loved working with Wayne Federman and watching him interact with Mulder and Scully was hilarious. The 'Running in High Heels' scene was hell on my wife Arlene. She had to do a lot of takes running her ass off back and forth in high heels, while Téa is on the phone in that scene, and she even tripped over a bunch of wires at one point. Luckily she is a fitness trainer so she was in very good shape and very capable. The bubble bath scene was interesting because we had to keep getting into the same bathtub, in the same water, and I was the last one to get in, after David or Gillian. They did keep adding warm water and bubbles, but I remember not being very happy, sharing the same funky bath water with two others. I also remember I had my daughter Sawyer, who was two or three at the time, on the set and she saw the zombies. She was not scared at all, but a couple of them walked by and she tells us, 'She's not pretty.' My wife and I laughed."

"This episode afforded us a great opportunity to explore *The X-Files* world," say Joy Krone and Adrienne Doucette. "Several of our friends were in town visiting, and we were able to get them on the show as extras. We sat in the movie theater and watched *The Lazarus Bowl* footage that was not used in the show or even the deleted scenes. For example, Téa Leoni and Garry Shandling were kissing in the coffin, but there was a string of saliva between their mouths. Everyone in the audience was completely grossed out. We wondered if David Duchovny showed that footage just to embarrass his wife. He seemed to be a really cool, easy-going director. At the end of the day, we were allowed to keep our *The Lazarus Bowl* programs. These were phony programs given to the audience members that had David Alan Grier's name and others listed as phony credits for the movie.

"The first scene we shot was at the premiere of *The Lazarus Bowl*," reminiscences fan Little Star. "They gave us the above programs as well as gold plastic bowls with the movie title's logo printed in gold on the side. The bowls had popcorn in them and we were told to eat and enjoy

Program cover to *The Lazarus Bowl*.
Photo by Adrienne Doucette.

"David came in dressed in a tux and looking fabulous," recalls Little Star. "He told us the plot of the episode and then showed us part of *The Lazarus Bowl*. It didn't have sound so David narrated it for us. David told us to react to the movie as if it's the greatest movie we'd ever seen. David was great as a director but someone should have told the Assistant Director (AD) that David is a very personal director. Before a scene, David addressed all the extras himself and told us exactly what to do. He then disappeared behind the monitors to watch the scene being filmed. The AD then came out and gave us the exact same instructions.

While he was still talking to us, David stepped out from behind the monitors and watched the AD with a bemused smile. When the AD finished, David stepped forward again to address us and said, 'So on this one...' everyone started laughing at the prospect of hearing the same thing for a third time."

"David had a lot of fun directing the extras," says Little Star. "When he shot our reactions to the movie he kept telling us it was the greatest movie we'd ever seen. Then he chose a few people to cry because the movie was such a beautiful love story. A few people he told to hold up the program like they were looking for the name of one of the smaller actors. He told the entire group of us when to clap, when to cheer and when to give the movie a standing ovation. He then chose several people, seemingly at random, to not react at all. He told them to just sit, watch the movie and not react. Just before shooting a scene, several people surrounded David to fuss about his appearance. They fixed his hair, touched up his makeup and smoothed out his tux. With a smile David joked, 'See how many people it takes to make me look half way descent.' He got a laugh from the crowd so he continued his joking. 'There are whole teams. It starts at my house, they're in my car.' Again, more laughter followed."

"Mitch then came in dressed in a tux and looking spiffy," continues Little Star. "He sat on the left hand side of the theater in the third row happily chomping on popcorn. His apparent date for the event was a twenty-something model. David had a great line when directing the Barbie girl how to react to Mitch. He was telling her to put her arm around him, turn her face toward him and give him a little kiss. Then he said, 'I'd like to demonstrate, but I won't.' David and Mitch joked around a lot and when David was ready to film, Mitch was still hamming it up. So David (still smiling) stepped back as if to wait and said, 'Whenever you're ready, Mitch.' Mitch wasn't the only person wanting to direct. After David yelled, 'Cut, that was a good one,' someone else came out from behind the monitors saying, 'No, no, no, this is all wrong.' It was Gary

Shandling announcing his arrival. The crowd was pleasantly surprised and enjoyed his joke."

"Gillian looked fabulous of course," continues Little Star. "She was wearing a sleeveless black dress and had her hair back in an adorable, black, sparkly headband. It may have been a ribbon since it was shoe-string thin. Shortly after Gillian had come in to film her scenes, David told the extras when to clap and cheer. Unfortunately, most of us couldn't hear him. So David and Gillian did their lines and David as Mulder stormed out of the theatre. It was silent. So Gillian turned to us and said 'Clap, guys, clap' which we then, of course, proceeded to do. I wish you could hear how she said it because it was just too damn cute! She also kept giggling."

"After several rehearsals and takes, they switched movies from *The Lazarus Bowl* to *Where the Heart Is* with Natalie Portman and Ashley Judd," continues Little Star. "David addressed the extras again after several more had been brought in. He told us how to react and then said, 'Enjoy the movie. It stars Natalie Portman and Rene Russo.' Everyone remained silent even though Ashley Judd was staring back at us from the screen. This is when my alternate personality, the obnoxious one, took control of my mouth and I said, 'Ashley Judd.' He looked over at me and in his best Mulder deadpan said, "Yeah, I'm a big fan." The crowd loved it. Much later after all the big names came in to shoot their cameos, David told them what to do. Then he said, 'Enjoy the movie. I don't know what it is but Natalie Portman is in it.'"

"Some of the highlights of the day for me were when I got to take pictures with David, take pictures in Mulder's office and take pictures in Scully's apartment," concludes Little Star. "It was all very surreal."

Mulder's office. Photo by Adrienne Doucette.

"We were also allowed to tour Mulder's office and Scully's apartment, continue Joy Krone and Adrienne Doucette. "We got to sit in Mulder's chair, take pictures of the bookshelves, and sit on Scully's couch. That was a really cool experience. We were in such a panic to take pictures of everything in the limited amount of time that we had, so it was hard to take it all in. We remember that the hallway outside of *The X-Files* office was piled with crap. Some of the things that we saw in those piles were books on fatherhood and anatomy, which kind of gave a clue as to what would happen later on in the season. There were also some strange trophies, books that didn't belong, and a basketball. Fans might be pleased to know that Mulder's pencils remained permanent fixtures in the ceiling, and we were amused by that as well. In Scully's apartment, she had a really intricate china cabinet in her kitchen. All the place settings were there, a whole bunch of different glasses, and these beautiful glass cabinets."

7x20 Fight Club

Written by: Chris Carter
Directed by: Paul Shapiro
Summary: Doppelgangers Beth and Lulu try to avoid each other, but end up moving to the same city over and over. Whenever they meet mayhem follows and people caught between them are likely to break out in uncontrollable violence. When the women fall in love with the same man, wrestler Bert, they both refuse to move away. Scully discovers that they have the same father and their powerful connection might have to do with him being the world's angriest man. She also finds that Bert has a doppelganger, just like the two women. When they all come together at Bert's wrestling match all hell breaks loose. Mulder and Scully do not escape unharmed.

Lulu's Koko's Copy Center
1201 W. 5th St.
Los Angeles, Ca

Wrestling Match
Grand Olympic Auditorium
1801 S. Grand Ave.
Los Angeles, Ca

"[My daughter] Sawyer was on set when my wife Arlene and Steve Kiziak were wrapped up in traction at the beginning of *Fight Club*," continues Mitch. "Well, Sawyer comes in and she sees her mommy in the hospital bed, so she walks over and pats her hand and says, 'It's okay Mommy. It's okay.' Having Sawyer, and Piper exposed to that kind of stuff lets them see what Daddy and Mommy did for work. It was the norm for them."

Mitch Pileggi enlightened me as to how entertaining it was working with his wife, Gillian's double, on the show. "My secretary would walk in to tell Skinner something in a particular scene and she would burst out laughing and would say, 'I just walked in here and you're not Mitch!' She would laugh every time and I had to tell her she could not do that when we were acting. She eventually got it. Sometimes Arlene would do 2nd unit if Gillian was not available; there were times when I was doing my scene with Arlene, where they shot her from behind for my coverage. It did not happen often, but I do recall it happening."

"I just feel that we missed some opportunities with *Fight Club*," says Chris Carter. "I don't know if I would do it over completely, but I think there were things that could have been better thinking back to it."

"As we walked inside the entrance to the Grand Olympic Auditorium, fans were each handed a 5 inch by 7 inch white envelope, numbered and stamped with THE X-FILES in small black print," shares fan Apollina92. "The envelope contained: a small pack of peanuts; a small pack of 4 chewy sweets; 1 raffle ticket; an orange sheet with instructions and information; a program for the 'wrestling match'; and a white Indemnification and Release form. Also as we were walking inside, we each had the back of our right hands stamped with THE X-FILES in bold blue capital letters."

Fight Club Wrestling Match Program. Photo by Little Star.

"The first scene to be filmed was Mulder coming down the steps to the left of the wrestling ring," Apollina92 excitedly continues. "One doppelganger of Kathy is already standing near the ring. Mulder starts talking to this doppelganger, but I couldn't hear what he was saying. Then a second Kathy starts walking towards the wrestling ring. For this scene, and all the scenes that Mulder is in, David Duchovny (and his double) was wearing a dark grey or black suit, with the white shirt not tucked into his trousers, and a blue tie. One of the Kathy's, I think the second one, was wearing a pink vest, over a grey (I think) t-shirt, and dark trousers."

"When this scene had finished filming, Dave, who was our MC (guy who entertained us in between filming, with jokes, trivia questions, and raffles, etc) walked through us fans (the audience) asking trivia questions and giving away black *The X Files* t-shirts to the fans who first responded correctly in their section," Apollina92 carries on. "He also asked who was from out of town, and where each out-of-towner was from. Fans had come from New Zealand, Australia, South Africa, and around the USA. I got the chance to say that I was from London, England, but was currently living in Minneapolis."

"The second scene to be filmed was the wrestling match between the two wrestlers, Texx Cobb and the Van Daminator," she continues. "The scene also involved Mulder picking up the first Kathy doppelganger, throwing her over his left shoulder, and then putting her down next to the wrestling ring. During this scene, we, the crowd, had to pantomime cheering and watching the wrestling match. There was a bit during the match when Texx throws the Van Daminator down on the ring floor. By the second or third take, we had unspokenly decided to jump up from our seats at this point, and punch the air. It looked really good, even though we were being quiet! Then we were asked to pantomime fighting. We did this once. But then the guy giving us directions asked us to pantomime *gradually* starting to fight. We did this, many, many times, including many people throwing popcorn, which they had been given in bags. While we were 'fighting,' male ushers walked down the aisles, each with a tray of empty cups of Coca Cola. All this 'fighting' was going on while the wrestlers were wrestling in the ring, and Mulder throwing the first Kathy doppelganger over his left shoulder, her yelling something, then Mulder bringing her closer to the wrestling ring, and then putting her down, there."

"Then we were all asked to move seats," chuckles Apollina92. "My section moved left, and lower down, that is, closer to the stage area. While we were moving, some fans started saying, 'Moooo' and 'Baaaah,' which I thought was very funny, since we were indeed being moved like cattle!"

"We pantomimed fighting again," Apollin92 keeps on. "Mulder lifted the first Kathy and threw her over his left shoulder. This time, however, he moved her to the right hand side of the stage. We filmed this scene several times. When it was a cut, the announcer giving us our directions and instructions announced that the next scene to be filmed would feature Gillian Anderson. The crowd went wild, including me! I think that we went even more wild than when David Duchovny came on stage. Then we moved back to our original seats. Gillian Anderson's double, Michelle Chaldu, then came and stood on the steps in the aisle to my right. Her likeness to Gillian is uncanny, but if you look at her face closely, you can tell that it's not Gillian. Gillian's double was wearing a black trouser suit. Then we were given more instructions, but no filming took place."

"Then we did the next scene: us gradually fighting, then Gillian and Texx Cobb walking down the steps in the aisle to my right," shares Apollina92. "Then Scully and Texx stop just below my seat level. Texx sees his doppelganger in the wrestling ring on the stage, then looks amazed to see his doppelganger. We the audience crowd look to the stage; we then also look amazed to see the Texx doppelganger in the wrestling ring. Texx then growls, and breaks free of his chains, and rushes towards the stage. But then the scene cuts, so he doesn't get anywhere near the wrestling ring. Scully looks at Texx, shocked; he almost knocks into her. We resume 'fighting,' as Texx rushes towards the stage. We filmed this scene over and over and over again, which was good for me, because I got to see Gillian Anderson walking up and down the aisle steps to my right lots of times."

"When that scene was a cut, Gillian had to leave," states Apollina92. "She went down to the stage area, and thanked everyone and said that she had to leave now. She said that David Duchovny was still here (quote: 'At least I think David's still here.') But Dave the MC, said that he had told Gillian that a lot of people had come from out of town, so she stayed a bit longer, and signed a few autographs, which was very nice of her."

"After she left, we moved again; again, my section moved to the left and lower down, closer to the stage, to similar seats to where we sat when we had moved seats earlier," continues Apollina92. "We filmed the scene of us pantomiming cheering and watching the wrestling match, and Mulder throwing the first Kathy doppelganger over his left shoulder, her yelling, and him taking her from one side of the ring to the other. I had a great side view of David Duchovny! But when this scene was a cut, David was done for the day. He thanked us for our patience and said that we had been a great crowd. His voice sounded a little hoarse; then he left. He waved a little as he was leaving. He got a pretty big cheer, but not quite as big as the cheer that Gillian Anderson had received. Kathy Griffin also left around this time."

"Next, Producer Harry Bring was introduced to us by Dave, the MC," shares Apollina92. "Harry thanked us for coming out, and told us to look for ourselves on TV on May 7th. Dave then asked more trivia questions, with black *The X Files* t-shirts as prizes once again. One girl knew the case file number of Scully's abduction X-File case. She got a t-shirt *and* a signed black and white 8 inches by 10 inches photograph of Mulder and Scully."

"I flew back home the following day," recalls Apollina92. "The hilarious thing is that the exact same day as the *Fight Club* event the following year, Monday 9th April 2001, I attended a Buskaid Concert at the University of California, Los Angeles hosted by Gillian Anderson. I went with my friend, C. We sat next to Steve Martin at the concert. C sat next to him, on his right, and I was on her right. Gillian was directly behind us. The Buskaid children were fantastic: playing a classical music concert without sheet music! The next day, Tuesday 10th April 2001, C, myself, and a few other friends went to try and see the filming of the 8th series finale, *Essence* and *Existence*, but that's a whole other story."

Prop money used in *Fight Club*. Photo by Little Star.

"This episode was the open call for [500] Philes from all over the world to come," fan LizzyX tells me. "People from Russia, Japan, and Germany came to be extras on the show. I had just turned 18 and had told my Mom I was going to spend the weekend at my friend's house. Instead, I hoped on a bus that same night from Texas and went to meet up with a girl whom I had met from the Internet. I didn't know anything about her; I just knew that she was picking me up at the Los Angeles Greyhound and I had no idea who this person was. I was just going to stay at her place and go to this filming. Thank God she was really nice, and did not turn out to be some sort of serial killer. To this day, my Mom doesn't know what I did!"

"It was a long shoot, like 16 hour days," recalls LizzyX. "The first two nights was just pretty much David and Kathy Griffin and it was pretty funny since [they] were joking around and watching the fans. David went up to these two girls, and one of them was doing [a headlock] and David started laughing. They were really great to us."

"When Gillian finally came to the set, we went crazy," LizzyX says excitedly. "As soon as Gillian Anderson walked out, people gave her a standing ovation. This was the weekend that Gillian's episode aired so everyone had posters saying *'We loved all things'* and *'Congratulations'*. They went crazy and she was kind of laughing. It was her first day of the shoot and she shot with the fans that were not paid, while David was shooting with the fans that were paid. He got a little worried since she was working with the fans that had never done this before; hadn't done extra work, were overzealous fans, and didn't know how to act [around actors] and she was the one who was picked to be in the middle of that crowd. He was very vocal about this on set. There was a point during the shoot where she was talking to the director and she was like, 'I'm ok. I'm fine. It's ok. They're not going to hurt me.' I remember her being tiny, like super, super tiny and her clothes fit really big on her. When they called it a wrap, Gillian and David were walking away together and everyone was like 'GILLIAN' so she came back around and signed autographs."

"There was a large fan call for this episode in an effort to reward the fans and use them as extras in the wrestling auditorium, much like the large call they had in Vancouver during the filming of the chess scene in *The End*," shares Adrienne Doucette. "The auditorium was filled to the brim with excited X-Philes from all over. There were a lot more crew hired for this episode and they had a comedian entertaining the fan side and they had trivia questions and t-shirt giveaways. They treated the fans really well, and the fans did a great job acting, as well as the extras, if not better since they REALLY wanted to be there. They were served pizza for lunch, all day for free, but it was long seventeen-hour day. The fans were troopers and I hope many of them received t-shirts out of the trivia game. We had to pretend to cheer (silently, of course, as not to interrupt filming). I remember David Duchovny looking straight at me when I was doing my phony cheer, and he just burst out laughing and gave me the most beautiful smile. I was so thrilled. I did have a bad experience though. In the scene where the twins get near each other, the audience members had to pretend that we were fighting with each other. I ended up accidentally hitting my friend, Little Star, in the eye and sliced her contact lens in half. I felt so bad because she had to leave for a few minutes to fix her contact lens and by the time she came back she had missed Gillian Anderson appearing to the fanatically cheering crowd. The fans held up signs saying how much they loved *all things* and how appreciative they were to be there and have this experience. The fans were the ones that instigated the cheers to Gillian and she seemed really touched that they knew about it."

"It is such a thrill walking up to a security guard or a PA and saying, 'Hi, I'm here to be an extra on *The X-Files*.' No matter how many times you get to say it, it's always awesome," says Little Star. "Anyway, Friday was very, very long. We shot for 16 hours. Much of that time was spent cheering (silent and aloud) and dodging popcorn that kept flying through the air. Some guy three rows in front of me kept letting the popcorn fly every time he cheered. The rest of us groaned when the Props Manager handed him several bags of popcorn and told him to keep it up. We couldn't believe he was encouraging this mess. By the end of the evening, the popcorn was so thick on the ground it was ridiculous. When the crowd breaks into fighting, we were slipping around as if we were fighting on an ice rink. They finally put some kitty litter down which helped a little."

"The fighting was fun," excitedly shares Little Star. "The Production Assistant's (PA) kept saying 'Safety is no accident' and we all had a great time pantomiming our fights. Apparently not everyone heard the motto because somebody broke a finger."

"The first scene we shot was David walking down from the crowd and approaching Kathy Griffin," recalls Little Star. "Two of my friends and

I had prime seats. We were sitting in the front row on the aisle that David walked past. We had one practice rehearsal, pantomiming our cheers then we were ready to shoot with David. David looked right at my friend and me and laughed while we rehearsed. As David walked to his starting position, he walked right past us so I took the opportunity to say, 'Hey David, your new movie is really funny.' Several people in the crowd agreed with me and he looked at me and said, 'Oh thanks!' He then commented about the level of enthusiasm we had and then said, 'Just wait till ten hours from now. You won't love it as much.' I informed him, 'We were here for sixteen hours on Friday.' He looked surprised and said, 'Really? And you're back?'"

"In the next scene, Kathy Griffin approaches her doppelganger David then picked up Kathy's body double and carried her away over his shoulder," laughs Little Star. "Being silly, instead of putting Kathy down after a take, he held her like a football and ran back to position with her under his arm. After they had that scene, they shot it again this time with Kathy and her body double switching places. I thought it was interesting that the script supervisor said the lines instead of the body double. Anyway, this time David picked up Kathy and carried her away. During rehearsals Kathy yelled at her twin, 'I'm gonna kick your ass, bitch!' For the actual take, she yelled, 'I'm gonna kick your butt from here till Tuesday!' and variations on that line."

"Throughout the day we got to fight several times," recalls Little Star. "We were of course stage fighting so we never got hurt. However, just before Gillian showed up, my good friend jammed her finger through my eye. The irony here is that we were not fighting at the time. She tripped and my eye broke her fall. If that wasn't painful enough, half of my contact came out. While I was trying to find the other half of my contact swimming around in my eye, Gillian showed up. The roar was enormous. At this point, I didn't care if I couldn't find my contact and I was half-blind, I wanted to see Gillian. The AD asked the crowd if we liked Gillian's episode the night before and the crowd went wild."

"Then it was time to shoot the scene," says Little Star. "I must say Gillian was very brave because she stood in the section where all the free people were sitting and while she was there, the crowd breaks into fighting. It looked pretty out of control and after reading several other peoples accounts of their day; it apparently was out of control. I've read that people were sore and bruised. All too soon Gillian was done and ready to leave. She took the mike from Bear (the AD) and addressed the crowd. She said she had to leave but before she did she signed autographs for a bunch of people. Instead of pushing through the mob scene, I waited for Gillian out by her trailer. She changed into a little white shirt, black Capri pants and tan sandals. She looked very cute. As she walked to her car there were about five fans waiting for her. Someone said, 'Awesome episode last night.' She turned from walking to her car to come over to where we were and said, 'Did you like that?' She seemed very pleased and willingly signed autographs for everyone waiting."

"Anyway, I went back inside to finish filming and after one more scene we were done. Driving with only one contact was rather terrifying but I made it home safely," concludes Little Star. "An hour and a half later, I found the other half of my contact still in my eye. Those of you with contacts understand the agony of losing a contact in your eye. All is well though, my eye is healed and I can see again; although, I'm seriously considering getting one of those laser eye surgeries."

> The cast and crew of
>
> the X-Files
>
> wish to thank you
>
> for helping
>
> to make this a
>
> great episode.
>
> **X-FILES**

A thank you to the fans from the cast and crew.
Photo by Little Star.

"We saw them film at the copy center where one of Kathy Griffin's character was going to get a job," Kathleen Keegan tells me. "That was an interesting location since it was downtown and directly across the street and below the building they used as the Dallas Federal Building in *Fight the Future*. Whenever there was a successful take, the whole crew would yell, 'WOOOO!' really loud. It was their thing for the day. Towards the end of the day, from our vantage point, we were able to watch them film the stunt that Mulder does down in the manhole in the middle of the street. All day long, the crew was talking about this stunt and David was not looking forward to it. They took the manhole cover off, and David places his butt in the rim of the manhole and he does the back flip out of the hole. The first time he did that, the flip was crooked and he fell to the side. He did it again and it was perfect so they wrapped for the night. When we finally saw the episode, we were so disappointed because they didn't even leave that in there. It looked so cool when David did it, but it was cut. When we watched them film these scenes, we were able to sit on the stairs on the Federal Building, but when I went back years later, that area where we sat is now a film studio and it's gated off. "

"I didn't think I was going to get to go," shares Julie Cantrell. "When I first read on the Official X-Files Website that an episode was being filmed and all Philes were invited, I was ecstatic. Only one little problem; the filming was to take place in downtown Los Angeles and I live in Ohio. However, being the persistent fan that I am, I managed to finagle a couple of plane tickets and some time off of work so I could have the experience of my Phile life. So, accompanied by my dear friend, Wendy, I headed west."

"The filming for *Fight Club* was to start at 11:00 AM on Monday April 10, 2000 and I wanted to get there early," continues Julie. "We arrived at the Grand Olympic Auditorium around 9:30 AM and there was already a significant line. There were quite a few crew members around and a lot of activity was taking place behind the building, but no one could really see anything. We stood for quite a while chatting amicably with a couple of people when a security guy came around and informed everyone that everyone would be searched and no cameras would be permitted. He said that if anyone had a camera, it would be confiscated at the door. I was slightly irritated because I didn't trust these goons with my camera. So, I had decided that when we went in, I'd offer them my camera batteries."

"We stood for a little longer when a couple of crew members came around asking how we had heard about it," resumes Julie. "I told them I read it on the internet and hopped on a plane. They asked where we were from and we told them. They then wanted to know if we had flown in just for the filming. When we answered affirmatively, they gave us that little, 'Wow, you guys are nuts' look while their mouths said, 'Wow, that's cool.' They walked down a little further then came back. One of them handed us a call sheet and said, 'here; not too many people get these.' I nearly laid down and died right there."

"By noon, we were let in and seated," continues Julie. "On a side note, I went through two security guards and neither one said a darn thing about my camera. We were each given an envelope containing a bag of Planters peanuts, a Tootsie roll, an indemnification & release form that was to be signed (which no one collected), and a sheet with explanations about the episode and directions, etc. We were told that if we had to go to the bathroom, we'd have to ask one of the many P.A.'s wandering around."

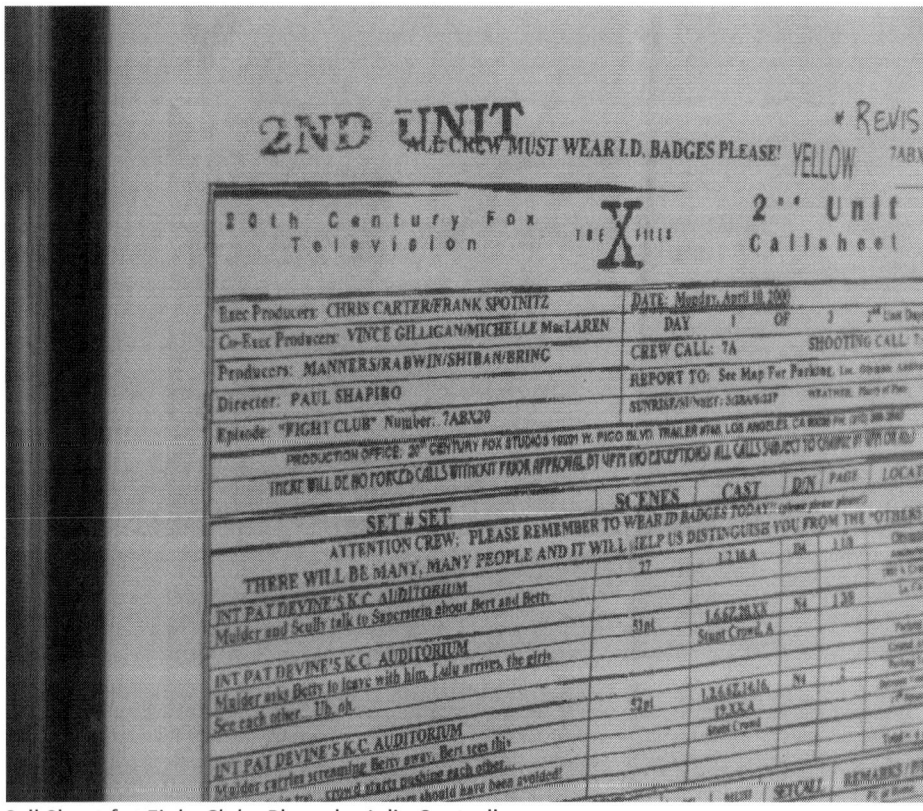

Call Sheet for *Fight Club*. Photo by Julie Cantrell.

"The room was dark and smoky, courtesy of the fog machines," states Julie. "Each entrance at the top of the stairs had bright lights shining through them making a cool silhouette of whoever walked through."

"We were introduced to comedian Dave, who knew next to nothing about *The X-Files*, but managed to keep us from getting too restless," resumes Julie. "Then, Assistant Director Barry Thomas (or 'Sugar Bear' as he informed us) began explaining to us what we'd be doing as the audience. This crew was the 2nd Unit Crew. The 1st Unit Crew was already working on Episode 21, *Je Souhaite*. Before he got too far into the explanation, many of us noticed David Duchovny walking down the ramp on the opposite side of the auditorium. Whispers of 'there he is!' and 'oh, my God! were heard here and there. Finally, a few braver souls started giving little squeals of delight. Noticing that he had lost us, Barry said, 'Okay. Everyone say 'Good morning, David,' which we all chimed to say. He shyly smiled at the audience and gave a little half-wave."

"For the first couple of shots, we just sat there because they were filming on the other side of the auditorium," adds Julie. "It was our jobs to be very, very quiet. The extras on the other side had to 'pantomime' like they were watching a wrestling match. David walked up the stairs until we could not see him anymore. When the director yelled, 'action' he re-entered with the light behind him giving that cool silhouette I was talking about earlier. He walked down the stairs and behind Kathy Griffin. I could barely hear him, but I did hear the words, 'Fox Mulder from the FBI.' Just hearing that in person was a dream come true for me."

"Later, they moved us on the other side of the auditorium," continues Julie. "On that side, I was pretty close to the front and got a good look at David getting his hair done. Let me just say this: 'YUM!' The man is sexier in person. Television does nothing for the real deal. He is truly the most elegant looking man I've ever had the pleasure of looking upon. I really got the impression that he was very professional and did his job quite well despite the hundreds of women drooling over him."

"When ready for the next shot, the audience was told to 'behave' around Gillian," states Julie. "No one was to ask for autographs, handshakes, or pictures. We were told to think of it as work and we had to do what we were told. Gillian climbed the stairs next to our section. A few people made little 'woo-hoo' sounds and she tried to keep a straight face. I think she may have been a little bit embarrassed by the attention. Anyway, in a similar fashion to David, she came down the stairs with a security guard and Bert Zupanic's look-alike, who happens to be an inmate in shackles. As they come down the stairs, the audience is supposed to be fighting. Once they made the entrance, we were to stop fighting, look at the inmate with Gillian and then at the ring at Zupanic. The inmate breaks his chains and races down the stairs and the audience was to start fighting again. This scene was shot a few times. An interesting side note, when Gillian comes down the stairs she was given direction to 'make eye contact with David' and also, to 'gloat.' Once, she was way off of her mark and everyone chuckled. But, she took it all in stride and did her job."

"Like David, Gillian Anderson is even better looking in person," raves Julie. "She's a very stunningly beautiful woman and a heck of a lot smaller than you'd think. She's a tiny person and it's hard to imagine her kicking anyone's butt. She was wearing the classic Scully suit with black slacks and long jacket. After her scene, Gillian left, but signed as many autographs as she could as fast as she could before she left, then tossed the Sharpie pen she was using in the audience. I realized too late that she was giving autographs, so I missed out. I was just thrilled to see her, though. Before she left, she thanked the audience for being there and supporting the show and asked that everyone stick around for David."

"Once again, we were shuffled around and watched David pick Kathy Griffin up some more," continues Julie. "Before too long, he left as well. Like Gillian, he said thanks to the audience especially for fighting so well."

"We stuck around to the end and watched the photo doubles and the wrestlers for their final scenes," adds Julie. "Around 9:00 PM, it was called a day. Barry thanked everyone for coming and told everyone we did a good job. Exhausted and thrilled, Wendy and I were deflated once we realized we were stuck in downtown L.A. with no transportation. We tried calling a cab, but didn't know which service to call or anything. Needless to say, we were creeped out. We asked one of the security guards from the auditorium what we should do. His answer was that we were in the ghetto and there were no cabs in that part of town. He then snidely wished us good luck. Lucky for us, a fellow Phile, Diane McDonald, had returned to pick up a prize she had won in the raffle. She so kindly gave us a ride to our hotel. Both Wendy and I are forever grateful to her."

"So, we spent all day watching the filming that will probably result in two minutes of the entire episode," finishes Julie. "I really have so much more respect for these people who spend such long hours to give us quality entertainment. They're a professional group of people who really work their butts off. I really had a blast and I am hoping for another season so I can do it again next year."

7x21 Je Souhaite

Written by: Vince Gilligan
Directed by: Vince Gilligan
Summary: Anson Stokes has unrolled a jinniyah with an attitude from within an old carpet and has been granted three wishes. He's not having much luck with his wishes and ends up invisible and dead. Eventually Mulder unrolls the jinniyah and gets his three wishes.

Gen's Café
Elysee Café
1099 Gayley Ave.
Los Angeles, Ca

"I preferred scouting locations for the stand-a-lone episodes," says Ilt Jones. "I'm not a huge sci-fi fan. That being said, I loved the ingenuity of some of the stand-a-lone episodes. I always wondered what they were going to come up with next. My favorite episode that I worked on was *Je Souhaite* (7x21). I found it hilarious; it was brilliantly clever and I loved Mulder's three wishes. In fact, for his first wish, where he wishes for peace on Earth, we closed down ten blocks of Spring St. and eight blocks of 6th St. in downtown Los Angles early on a Sunday morning. We had about a hundred PA's and about twenty police officers and we were able to place a bus, halfway across an intersection, bicycles and briefcases all over the place, to make it look like the people had just vanished. That was one of my favorite shots."

"Gillian asked me to be in *Je Souhaite* with her as one of the scientists to see the invisible body in the morgue," recalls Harry Bring. "I do a few little side gags, like buck teeth and thick 'Coke Bottle' glasses, and she wanted me to wear those for the scene. We actually did one take with those glasses and then we did another without them."

7x22 Requiem

Written by: Chris Carter
Directed by: Kim Manners
Summary: Mulder and Scully return to Oregon where they worked on their first case together. A UFO has collided with a military aircraft and the Cigarette Smoking Man, who is very ill and hopes to rebuild the project, sends Krycek to recover it. Abductees are being taken and, afraid that Scully will be taken as well, Mulder refuses to let her go with him to find the UFO. She sends Skinner with him instead, but realizes that it is

not abductees that are being taken - it's people who have experienced the same kind of brain activity. Mulder is abducted right in front of Skinner's eyes and Scully learns she is pregnant.

Cuddle Motel
41693 Big Bear Blvd.
Big Bear Lake, Ca

Author's Note: My friends and I took a day trip up to Big Bear for these locations. The weather was beautiful, the company engaging, and the scenery gorgeous. As we parked to forage for lunch, we came across a giant X, painted right on the ground. It was not orange, nor near the main road, but our excitement increased and photographs were taken.

Season Eight: Changing of the Guard

The premiere of *The X-Files* eighth season marked a dramatic change for the show. With Fox Mulder's abduction, Dana Scully was left feeling bereft, and surprisingly, with child. Composer Mark Snow created an evocative piece of music, which perfectly encompassed her inner struggle. "In making *Scully's Theme*, Chris had called me about something he had heard that was just a simple synth cord or pad solo signing and I thought how perfect it would be," recalls Mark. "I forget the name of the song but I thought how perfect it would be for Scully's theme. So much of the later seasons were her isolated from Mulder. I thought it was appropriate that it be the female vocal, a vocal morphing of the words, where the words were not pronounced but subliminally there. There were times where it sounded almost Middle Eastern; those were happy accident. I do remember that piece getting a lot of attention, showing up on You Tube."

While Fox Mulder might have been missing in action, Dana Scully was certainly not alone. Mitch Pileggi's Walter Skinner saw more screen time, and Season Eight also allowed for the return of Mrs. Margaret Scully. While it is hard to imagine anyone other than the wonderful Sheila Larkin playing the Scully matriarch, had Producer R.W. Goodwin been in charge of casting, a different actress would have been cast. "David [Nutter] had come up to me and said that my wife, Sheila Larken, would be perfect to play Scully's mom in *Beyond the Sea*," R.W. tells me. "I frankly did not agree with him since Sheila looked too young to be Scully's mother. So I told him that he and Chris [Carter] would have to cast that part."

"He said I was too young? Isn't he sweet!" replied Sheila Larken when informed of her of her husband's comment. "In truth, I think I was the right age and I am the same age as Gillian's mom, but I think Gillian looked more mature than her age and I probably looked younger than my age. I didn't feel that I was too young for the part, but I'm glad he did. I'm so glad he was not responsible for the casting; thank God for Chris Carter and David Nutter. *The X-Files* was an amazing show, and now that you're bringing all these back up, I'm realizing how many episodes I did with Kim."

The character of Margaret Scully has been a fan favorite since her appearance in season one. When asked why the fans always felt a special connection to Mrs. Scully, Sheila had this to say: "I always felt that Margaret Scully was a woman of incredible faith, a real Catholic and a real believer," replies Sheila. "This was the core that she always clung to and that is where she found her inner strength. Margaret would lose her temper when she got scared. That's when parents lose their temper; when they get scared, when they think that their child is in danger. I think that's why everyone likes Margaret Scully, because she is the ideal therapist mother. She helps you focus on your thoughts; encourage you to act on them."

With David's departure from the series, the dynamic of previous seasons was shifted. Season Eight saw a change in the relationship of Skinner, Scully, and Mulder, in particular. "Working on *The X-Files* was always physically challenging, and mentally challenging to prepare for that amount of work on a daily basis; for ten months out of the year, to know that a large amount of people were watching; to know that it was not something you could do automatically," reminisces David. "Each show had its own demands, whether it was in tone or physicality or both. It was constantly shifting and changing and in that way it was always interesting, but also tiring after nine years. The nature of the show is that it was able to flex and run through many genres, from comedy to horror, mystery to sci-fi to drama, so depending on what tone we were in, the Skinner/Scully/Mulder relationship was going to change, or parts of the relationship would come forward, while other parts would recess. I think it's fair to say that Skinner was the boss of Mulder and Scully and he had a certain fondness for the two of them and you could interpret it as coming from an older brother, although Mitch might point out that he is not that much older."

"I think Skinner was a big brother figure to Mulder and Scully over the years," adds Mitch Pileggi. "He was very much an ally; he felt responsible for them before and after Mulder was abducted. He wanted to protect them and make sure they are okay. I think Skinner felt guilty, especially when he was around Scully. I know over the years they played this 'Skinner Has a Mad Crush on Scully' and I would kind of flavor scenes with her like that in the beginning."

Walter Skinner was not Mulder and Scully's only ally. The Lone Gunmen were also instrumental in assisting the dynamic duo in uncovering the truth. I asked the trio to describe the relationship between the boys and Mulder and Scully. "I think Mulder and Scully looked on the Gunmen in much the same way as the fans saw us: kind of funny, faithful, helpful," replies Bruce Harwood. "Initially I thought of Byers as looking on Mulder as sort of a lesser Gunmen, but the more we showed up on the show, the more Byers looked up to Mulder as the kind of person he would want to be. By the end, we were faithful sidekicks."

"I had certainly heard the terms 'Three Wise Men' when we were doing the show, but I never paid much attention until one of the crew members pointed it out," echoes Tom Braidwood. "We often referred to ourselves as the Three Amigos."

Concludes Dean Haglund, "you know that friend you have, who can always fix your computer, and wire up your home theater, but is a little odd and always calls to see what you are doing, but you are always 'busy' or just heading out. And you never tell him to stop calling because you know one day you are going to update to Blu-ray and will need him to come over and hook it up, so you just put up with it? Yeah... we're that guy."

Allies may have returned, but so did some of the villains. The love to hate Alex Krycek was back, but not for long. "I got a call from Frank and Chris and they were very excited in letting me know that I was going to be killing Krycek, which made very happy," reports Mitch. "I was not happy that Nic was not going to be on the show anymore, but I was happy that I was chosen. Nic wanted David to kill him and I told him that if anyone has the right to kill you, it should be me, for all the pain and suffering I have had to go through because of your character. If he had to go, I was pleased it was me who put the bullet in his forehead, which looked pretty cool."

Veteran actor Robert Patrick was cast as Agent John Doggett, who was in charge of the search for the missing Fox Mulder. His introduction to both Dana Scully and the viewers at home is memorable. "We staged water in the face scene as the intro and shot it that way," Robert tells me when asked about his first scene. "It was the first scene I shot with Gillian and yes we did laugh about it."

Robert Patrick was not the only newcomer to Season Eight. Annabeth Gish was cast as the open-minded Agent Monica Reyes as a foil to John Doggett. When asked if she felt her character portrayed a softer side to that of Dana Scully, or if Agent Reyes was more feminine that Scully, Annabeth had this to say. "I would argue that Scully carried a lot of feminine energy," replies Annabeth. "Feminine and masculine strength can both be embodied and balanced in one character; softness too. Reyes seemed to bring open-minded, spiritual energy if you will. I remember Chris and Frank always used the word 'sunny' as an adjective for Reyes' additional outlook."

"*The X-Files* was significant for me professionally because it was the biggest show I've ever been a part of," continues Annabeth. "Working on *The X-Files* earned me a certain kind of badge, or a specialized degree of sorts. It's definitely a mark of pride for me. I loved Reyes from the moment I read her; her open-mindedness, her willingness to explore. I think empaths have great power, especially if they know how to wield the instinct positively. I think everyone has an ability to tap into a 'feeling' or a guidance system within. As for the show, they didn't need to exploit her abilities; it was just an aspect of her personality."

By Season Eight, the popularity of *The X-Files* was clearly known, all over the world. Director Michael Watkins told me about his travels overseas over the years. "I would travel through Europe, and I would get free dinners and wine because I had an *X-Files* T-Shirt or a hat and I would trade it," recounts Michael. "I had a woman sending me urine because she thought she was impregnated by an alien and she wanted it tested. It was a really intense job for me. It was hard to have fun when I was catching up every day."

Of course every episode that made it to television could not be hits. "*Baadla* was the one episode I did not like the most," producer Paul Rabwin says. "I think if I had to one episode to do different, it would be that one, and I would probably not do it. I think if I had done it different, I would have had John Shiban change the method of transportation. I don't think it ever worked on any level for me. It was weird and creepy, but I think the whole idea was distasteful to me. It's the only episode that I kind of wish we hadn't done."

There is a valid argument that the production work done on *The X-Files* made future shows like *Lost*, *Fringe* and *Bones* possible. "One of the cool things about *The X-Files* was that it pushed the envelope in terms of production value and what was being put out every single week," declares Mat Beck. "People really extended themselves. *The X-Files* was the first show I ever worked on where we started out shooting days, shot all night, and the last shots were days again. So one unit literally shot days, night, and days, but *The X-Files* were known for crazy hours. One of the things that would happen is the schedule would slip from day to day throughout the week. You might start off the first day of the week with a 7:00 call and by Friday your call was 4:30 in the afternoon. It was groundbreaking at the time, no question about that."

"My wife and I came up with an idea, that before we would start a season, we would have a big party at my house," declares Bill Roe. "It would be fifty to a hundred people there and it would be a 'Say Good-Bye To Your Loved Ones Weekend' because we were ready to start shooting *The X-Files* and we would not see our families for nine months. The hours were nice; start at seven o'clock Monday morning and then by Wednesday we would have a noon call and by Friday we would come home around seven o'clock in the evening and then start again Saturday morning. This happened for four years. I never would have thought I could do that for four years, but I'm glad I did. I'm glad I was asked back all those times and we all got along great."

"What made [working on *The X-Files* easy] was that we were doing real good work; it was really interesting stuff," proudly states Bill. "Nobody else was doing this sort of thing. Nobody will ever do anything like this again. We spent a lot of money, had all of the fun toys and had all the great stuff. What made it easy was being around all the great time. I think that was best and easiest part about working on the show. Working all night, working in cold and hot [temperatures] was not so fun, but it's part of the whole process. It's not very common that when you get home after working fourteen hours, all night long, and you're driving home at five or six o'clock in the morning you're saying to yourself, 'Wow, that was pretty cool.' That doesn't happen very often, but it happened on a regular basis with *The X-Files*. It was a life changing experience; to this day, it may be why so many folks talk about it all the time."

"The most difficult thing of doing *The X-Files* is that every week was another feature – it was huge. It was something very large that would happen in each episode, whether it was a hangar, out in the dessert, or out in the ocean, or on the docks," concludes Bill. "I never got to go on location scouting trips with directors. [My team] and I would have to rely on pictures, the directors, or rely on other crew members, which was fantastic, but not being there a week in advance was a little frustrating at times. While the cast and crew is rehearsing, while you're watching them set up, you start coming up with ideas and you do it. It's very quick and you don't have time to think about it. It was hard to show up at a place and say 'oh my goodness, what are we going to do now?' The directors knew how we worked, they knew what we wanted, and they were very prepared themselves. Pretty much everyone [in my team] was on the show for the whole four years that we did it here in Los Angeles, and I'm still using most of my crew now all these years later."

"Working on *The X-Files* certainly opened it up to a wonderful time and travel," shares Dean Haglund. "I still do conventions around the world, and as you know, still occasionally perform my one man improvised episode of *The X-Files*. But it is also that I meet real life conspiracy theorists and researchers that have taken me to some very interesting paths. Presently, a documentary film crew is following for the next 15 months as I come upon these stories and see where these events lead us, and how truth and conspiracy operate in our present day society. Look for that to come out in 2011 on Deanhglund.com.

"Working on *The X-Files* gave me confidence, so whatever was thrown at me would not be half as hard as *The X-Files* was," says Mac Gordon. "There has not been a show like that since it was on. It was edgy, unique, and expensive for television. We're not likely to see that again. I enjoyed walking into places, introducing myself, and presenting my card which had the grey X and the logo below it. People would look at that and it would open up so many more doors than any other show I had ever been on. Everybody in those days was an X-Files fan, so it was a tremendous advantage to have that card. People would ask me for my business card, and then ask for extras for their friends and family, just to have a piece of the show. Being a part of the show was fun. We had great people to work with which is a good thing because we spent way more time with each other than we did with our families. I enjoyed the crew; our producers were fun; the stories were fun. It was a cool experience to be a part of. That's my happy memory of it."

THE X FILES

Mac Gordon
Location Manager

10201 W. Pico Boulevard, Stage 5, Loft, Los Angeles, California 90035

Mac Gordon's X-Files business card. Photo by Mac Gordon.

"Some of the challenges that we faced on *The X-Files* were probably the fact that every episode was so different and such unique and original stories that were huge," Michelle MacLaren tells me. "Sometimes we were creating non-existent worlds, or matching to existing things that were huge."

The mythology episodes were the heart of *The X-Files* storyline. Staging a location for an alien crash or an alien landing could be difficult at times, but the crew always got it done. "Some of the stuff we did for the mythology episodes, like doing the UFO's, was always interesting because we would usually build an enormous light bar, anywhere from 30 to 50 feet, covered in lights, and then they would hang that off a huge crane and fly it out over the set, or wherever it was needed. That would be used for visual effects for them to paint an actual UFO around it, using the lights as the center of attention," says Tom Braidwood.

Chris Carter echoed many of the sentiments shared by the various directors over the course of the series. "My preference for directing was with stand-a-lones episodes, but there were times, like with *The Red and the Black*, it was so interesting to do a mythology episode, with all the special effects," Chris Carter tells me. "Then there were mythology stand-a-lones like *Duane Berry* and *Ascension*; I had a lot of fun doing that. I have to say that I did not have a preference directing types of episodes, but I did take more chances with the stand-a-lones than I did with the mythology episodes."

Season Eight was the first time writer and producer Frank Spotnitz directed an episode on *The X-Files*. A different challenge from what he was used to, Frank shares what the experience on *Alone* was like and how more seasoned directors on the show helped him. "I don't remember Kim giving me any specific advice about directing. By this time, I'd already learned an enormous amount from Kim and Rob, in particular, by watching the way they prepped episodes, listening to the questions they asked, and above all by helping to edit the film they had shot. There could be no better teachers. The filming of *Alone*, in particular, is one of my fondest memories. I do wish I had started directing sooner than I did."

Frank's crew gift to the crew for *Alone*: a bottle of wine from Stites private reserve, *Harvest Red: Liquefied for Easy Digestion.* Photo by Jana Fain

The season finale of this series left most viewers in shock: the return of Billy Miles, the death of Krycek, and the birth of William left fans with more questions than answers.

Season Eight Filming Locations

8x01 Within

Written by: Chris Carter
Directed by: Kim Manners
Summary: Following Mulder's disappearance, Deputy Director Kersh assigns Agent John Doggett to be in charge of the taskforce in search of Mulder. The investigation leads to Arizona with Scully, Skinner and Doggett's taskforce in pursuit of Gibson Praise, a boy who can read minds and may have alien physiology.

Split Mountain
Anza-Borrego State Park
Borrego Springs, Ca

"I remember a lot of late nights during the summertime and I was a kid, so I didn't have school, so I could work later," recalls Jeff Gulka. "I was pretty hot, but I remember a scene where Mitch had to carry me when I had my broken leg. We had to do that scene quite a few times and he was dying and sweating up bullets during that period. It was pretty funny since I didn't think he had it in him."

"It was really hot out in the desert and right before the scene where I carry Gibson, we had a company meeting of safety guys telling us there was a one in twenty five chance that one of us was going to get bit by a rattle snake," chortles Mitch Pileggi. "As I'm carrying Jeff, I have that going through my mind, and anytime on camera carrying anybody is hard, but Jeff was a great sport about it. He was very concerned about me carrying him, and of course he had grown quite a bit than he was when we first meet him in *The End*."

8x02 Without

Written by: Chris Carter
Directed by: Kim Manners
Summary: Doggett finds who he thinks is Mulder in the desert with Gibson. After 'Mulder' disappears again, Scully tells Doggett that it was not Mulder that he saw there but an alien bounty hunter disguised as him. The Bounty Hunter is looking to collect Gibson. Scully takes the boy to a hospital to be looked at where the bounty hunter tries again to take him but Scully kills him. Doggett becomes Scully's new partner on the X-Files.

School for the Deaf
Colorado Desert District Headquarters
200 Palm Canyon Rd.
Borrego Springs, Ca

Shooting Schedule
Thu, Aug 3, 2000

Page 17

Scene #93   **EXT - DESERT - Night**   6/8 Pgs

SCULLY is looking for something....and sees a light coming toward her.   N4

Cast Members
- 2. DANA SCULLY
- 2x. SCULLY ST DBL
- 50. STUNT COORDINATOR
- 54. HELO PILOT

Props
- BIG BEAM FLASHLIGHT(S)

Special FX
- Wetdown To Arrest Chopper Wash

Additional Crew
- HELO PILOT(S)

Art Dept/Set Dressing
- WILD GREENS OR BROWNS

Special Equipment
- CAMERA SHIP/HELO
- CAMERA MOUNTS
- NIGHT SUN
- FBI HELICOPTER

Version
Ep#2

Notes
HELICOPTER SAFETY BULLETIN

SPLIT MOUNTAIN

Wrap G.A. by 4am

Wrap at dawn or when work is done

END OF DAY #13 - 3 Total Pages

4pm leave from hotel

SHOOT DAY #14 -- Fri. Aug 11, 2000

Scene #48   **I/E - N.D. SEDAN/BURRO BEND CAFE - Day**   1 Pgs

SKINNER learns Gibson's whereabouts from people at Burger Stand...   D4

Cast Members
- 2. DANA SCULLY
- 3. A.D. SKINNER
- 17. ORDER TAKER
- 50. STUNT COORDINATOR

Extras
- 1 DROP DEAD GORGEOUS CHEF

Props
- PHOTOS OF YOUNG GIBSON

Visual FX
- RADIATION DISTURBANCE IN SCULLY'S POV
- VISUAL EFFECTS COORDINATOR

TBD

Scene #94   **EXT - DESERT - Night**   4/8 Pgs

SCULLY is struck with beam of light from above   N4

Cast Members
- 2. DANA SCULLY
- 2x. SCULLY ST DBL
- 50. STUNT COORDINATOR

Props
- BIG BEAM FLASHLIGHT(S)

Special FX
- Ritter Fans
- Wetdown To Arrest Chopper Wash

Additional Crew
- HELO PILOT(S)

Visual FX
- ADD STARS TO NIGHT SKY
- LOCKED OFF CAMERA FOR STARS
- VISUAL EFFECTS COORDINATOR

Art Dept/Set Dressing
- WILD GREENS OR BROWNS

Special Equipment
- CAMERA SHIP/HELO
- CAMERA MOUNTS
- NIGHT SUN
- FBI HELICOPTER

Version
Ep#2

Notes
HELICOPTER SAFETY BULLETIN

SPLIT MOUNTAIN

Shooting Schedule for *Within*. Provided by Patricia Steffy.

Driving out to the desert with a car full of Philes can have its advantages. This was one of those places where we did not have an exact address, just a general area. Using our combined X-Files knowledge, DVD's, and a laptop, we were able to map out the area. Once we found Gibson's school, we parked the car in the parking lot and began to photograph the building. A park ranger came over and asked us to move the car, to which my Canadian friend said she came all the way down from Canada to see the desert, and since there was no place to park with all the tourists here for the spring blooms, we would only like a few minutes with the desert beauty. He gave us a five minute window to snap our pictures, and then we were on our way with a thank you to him.

Gibson Praise's School for the Deaf. Photo by Erica Fraga.

Author's Note: If you feel the need to drive all the way down from Los Angeles, make sure you fill up on gas, water, and snacks. With the exception of motor homes, dirt bikes, and ATV riders, all you will find in Anza-Borrego is dirt and beautiful scenery, and limited cell phone service.

8x04 Patience

Written by: Chris Carter
Directed by: Chris Carter
Summary: When the body of a woman is pulled out of a river, the two agents go to Idaho where a human-bat is killing people. The woman was the wife of the man who caught the monster 40 years ago and had his scent on her. Anyone who has contact with the body is killed. Scully and Doggett track down the man who caught the creature which leads the monster to him, subsequently becoming targets after getting his scent on themselves.

Undertaker's Residence
Ventura Farms
235 W. Potrero Rd.
Thousand Oaks, Ca

Ernie Stefaniuk Residence
Golden Oak Ranch
19802 Placerita Canyon Rd.
Santa Clarita, Ca

8x05 Roadrunners

Written by: Vince Gilligan
Directed by: Ron Hardy
Summary: Scully gets stranded in Utah while investigating a missing persons case. The people of the town are members of a cult who put a parasitic organism into travelers to find The Second Coming. When the

current host dies, the townspeople put it into Scully. Doggett rescues Scully and cuts the organism out of her neck.

Cult Town
Four Aces Movie Ranch
E 145th and Ave. Q
Palmdale, Ca

8x06 Invocation

Written by: David Amann
Directed by: Richard Compton
Summary: A 7 year old boy named Billy who vanished 10 years ago mysteriously turns up having not aged at all. One of the suspects in Billy's disappearance was a teenager named Ronnie. After Doggett tells Ronnie he would like him to speak to Billy, Ronnie is startled by the knowledge that Billy is alive because he buried the boy many years ago. Billy's brother Josh is kidnapped by the same man and Ronnie leads the agents to the spot where Josh is hidden. Billy's ghost leads the partners to the dumping site of his bones.

"I was actually doing extra work for a movie called *Heart of the Champion* at the Grand Olympic Auditorium," LizzyX recalls. "I got a call from [a friend] at Central Casting who I had been begging to get me on *The X-Files*. He told me he got me something on *The X-Files* but that I had to be there at 2:00pm in Pasadena or someplace like that. I said, screw this, and literally walked away from my set! I didn't sign out or anything; I just left to go be on the *X-Files* set and I was in the Ferris wheel in the beginning of *Invocation*."

8x03 Redrum

Written by: Steven Maeda & Daniel Arkin
Directed by: Peter Markle
Summary: Martin Wells wakes up on Friday when he is being transferred out of a jail. When he wakes up the next day, it is Thursday. He meets Scully and Doggett who tell him that his wife has been murdered and he is the main suspect. As he moves backward through the week, he learns more about the murder, the murderer and how to save his wife.

Martin Wells Apartment
The Talmadge
3278 Wilshire Blvd.
Los Angeles, Ca

8x07 Via Negativa

Written by: Frank Spotnitz
Directed by: Tony Wharmby
Summary: A cult leader, Tibbett, believes he can see God by looking into the darkness within himself. Tibbett takes hallucinogens to reach a higher consciousness and kills his cult members by invading their nightmares. After Doggett meets Tibbett, he starts to have dreams with violent images and is afraid to sleep. He dreams he is going to kill Scully with an axe, but before he can, he turns the axe upon himself. Scully wakes him up, thus saving him from himself.

Cult House
837 Beacon Ave.
Los Angeles, Ca

8x08 PerManum

Written by: Chris Carter & Frank Spotnitz
Directed by: Kim Manners
Summary: A man named Duffy shows up at the office claiming that his wife is a multiple abductee who was killed by doctors after they stole her baby. The wife's situation closely resembles Scully's and makes her worry about her own pregnancy. After listening to Duffy's story, Scully believes she and another pregnant woman, Mrs. Hendershot, are in danger. She takes them to what she believes is a safe hospital to have the baby. When Scully realizes they are still in danger, she tries to get Mrs. Hendershot out of the hospital, but is intercepted by men who Scully later believes switched Mrs. Hendershot's baby with someone else's.

Late Night Diner
Tiara Café
121 E. 9th St,
Los Angeles, Ca

"During a birthing scene in *Per Manum*, the crew had trouble figuring out who was actually having the baby – Saxon Trainor, who played Mrs. Hendershot, or Kim," recalls Nina Jack of her time on Season 8. "If you ever watched Kim at the monitor, he had these certain poses, he would stand and his left arm would be bent; his right arm would be kind of straight; he would have this real intense look on his face; his eyes would be wide; he would nod his head and kind of shake a bit, especially when he was watching something really intense. Kim was a conductor. So, in the scene where Mrs. Hendershot was giving birth, Saxon was screaming with her labor pains. And there was Kim, screaming right with her."

"I was never on the set except for one time I acted in a scene in *Per Manum* as a silent doctor in a white coat, standing next to Gillian in some scene that was shot at night in the San Fernando Valley," recalls Mark Snow. "I remember how unbelievably boring it was; how hard these people work – the crew, the actors, the director. I think a lot of people don't realize how hard they all work and all they hear about is their salaries. It's really hard work. I remember the first time I came to California. My father –in-law, who was an actor in a series called *Medical Center*, invited me to the set. I was so excited about it. And about fifteen minutes later I said enough and wanted to leave. They would do these five second takes over and over again. I was used to getting a finished product that was edited into a final cut. After that experience, I had tremendous respect for the actors and the crew and how hard they worked at this, especially when they started at twelve midnight."

"My friend and I were outside of the diner with Kevin Cooper, David Duchovny's assistant," recollects Adrienne Doucette. "He was cracking jokes and entertaining us. It was a late night shoot in downtown Los Angeles and we were basically there because our cars were being used in the shot. Our friend, Little Star, was the waitress during the scene where Scully, Skinner, and Doggett are in the diner in the middle of the night. Doggett shows up, orders a cup of coffee, and Scully can't tell him that she's pregnant. We were stuck outside, but having fun regardless. My car was a gray 1986 Chevy Nova. When Doggett storms out of the cafe, you can see it parked across the street. There's a funny story here, actually. The Assistant Director sent a call out over the walkie-talkie requesting that the gray sedan across the street be moved up a little bit. Kevin had a walkie, so we all could hear the call. I told Kevin that they might mean my car, the Nova. As he was about to respond, someone answered over the radio, 'Do you mean the Lexus?' And the Assistant Director answered, 'No, it's not a nice car.' Everyone in our area laughed because they knew that meant they were talking about my car, the old Nova, which now the whole production knew of as 'not a nice car'."

"I arrived on the set early and met up with a friend of mine," Little Star tells me. "When transport came to pick us all up in the parking lot, the driver asked if one of us was the waitress. It was exciting to be the one who answered 'I am!' Out of all the extra work I've done, this was the first time I wasn't just another face in the crowd. We checked in then headed to wardrobe where they gave me a typical waitress dress. Next they shuffled us both over to hair and makeup. They spent about 15 minutes or more putting my hair up into some kind of twist. During that time the guest star of the week came in to have her hair done. Her name is Saxon Trainor according to the call sheet. Anyway, we sat and chatted while they worked on our hair and she talked about having to give birth on camera. When they were finished I headed back outside and ran into Mac Gordon, the locations scout. I hadn't seen him for a while so we chatted and caught up until Lisa, the person in charge of extras, came to fetch the two waitresses and the two chefs."

"She told me I would be behind the counter clearing away some dishes when Doggett would come in and ask me for some coffee before heading over to sit with Scully and Skinner. Michelle, Gillian's stand-in, and Mitch's stand-in were already seated at a nearby table," continues Little Star. "They were setting up the camera outside to shoot through the window so we just had to stand in our places to help them set up for the shot. During this, one of the extras came up to Michelle and asked to have his picture taken with her. Michelle paused for a moment, looking a little awkward then told him she wasn't Gillian. He was shocked, I don't think he really believed her because he kept staring at her and wouldn't leave. For those of you who haven't seen Michelle, she bares a very striking resemblance to Gillian. Many times on the set people have been excited when 'Gillian' walked by and I had to laugh because they had no idea it was Michelle. Anyway the guy wouldn't leave so I thought I'd jump in and help her. So I asked Michelle if this sort of thing happens a lot and she said yes. I asked her if she ever just said yes she was Gillian and she said never. Then we started making up headlines about the trouble that could be caused over Michelle impersonating Gillian. The guy finally left but I don't think he was entirely convinced he wasn't talking to Gillian."

"Gillian still wasn't around after we broke for a meal, but we did see Kevin," reminisces Little Star. "He's David's driver and a couple of my friends know him fairly well. So we chatted with him, asked him about David, and asked what he was doing here if David wasn't. He was sitting across from the Deli not too far away from two people I assume were X-Files fans who'd come to watch the filming."

"Finally it was time to start shooting again," Little Start begins again. "Mitch came in and took his place at the table. I've talked to him before, but it had been a long time. Then Gillian came in looking gorgeous. Someone asked if he could bring her anything and she asked for peppermint tea. She then took a look around the place and commented about the hanging lamps. They were very cool. No one knew if they belonged to the Deli or if the crew had brought them in. They were round and looked like paper mache string made out of glass."

"Kim Manners then came in and told Robert what he would be doing," recollects Little Star. "He was to walk up to me and ask me for coffee. Then Mitch pointed to the customer sitting at the counter and said, 'Then he's going to kick this guy's ass.' They laughed and said actually he would then go sit with Mitch and Gillian. He was also told that customer would be crossing in front of him. We rehearsed that a few times and it was very cool to have Robert Patrick look right into your eyes and ask you a question. Pure human reflexes made me answer him with a 'sure' or 'Um-hmm' every time he asked. They were filming through the window at this time so I didn't get in trouble for talking. They cut after Robert sat down with Gillian and Mitch, and every time he joined them they all burst out laughing. Kim came in once and told them not to laugh. That was shot a few times and once Kim actually came in and told me what to do! How cool is that, Kim Manners directed me."

"Next they shot Robert pulling up to the Deli and going in," continues Little Star. "Gillian and Mitch stayed where they were and talked to each other. I had to keep myself from staring and eavesdropping so I continued playing an IQ game and talking with the customer, the only other person in the Deli. The other waitress and the two chefs weren't in the scene so they were sitting in the next room. At one point, the customer and I were talking and we both started laughing. Gillian and Mitch looked up at us startled. I guess they thought we were eavesdropping so I apologized and went back to talking with the other extra. Color me embarrassed."

"Earlier Mitch had been joking with Robert that he was Mitch-a-phobic. Kim told Robert to pat Mitch's shoulder when he sat down as a 'hi, how ya doing' type greeting and Robert did it awkwardly then didn't do it at all," recollects Little Star. "Gillian and Mitch were laughing about that while Robert was filming outside. Then Gillian said something to the affect that Robert doesn't like to touch her either. She demonstrated what he does by using Mitch as herself. She stood up and put her hand on his back like she was looking over his shoulder at something then awkwardly removed her hand and stood as if she didn't know what to do with her arms, finally crossing them. They both laughed. So Robert isn't a touchy type person."

"The next scene they shot next was Doggett storming out of the Deli, Scully following him, they talk, then Skinner joins them," continues Little Star. "In between takes, Mitch and Gillian came back in the Deli to wait for their cue. There was a bowl of candy and Gillian popped one in her mouth. Of course I too had to eat one. I also grabbed one to keep as a souvenir. Everyone had one or two during the course of the night and a debate ensued over what the flavor was. Butterscotch of some sort won."

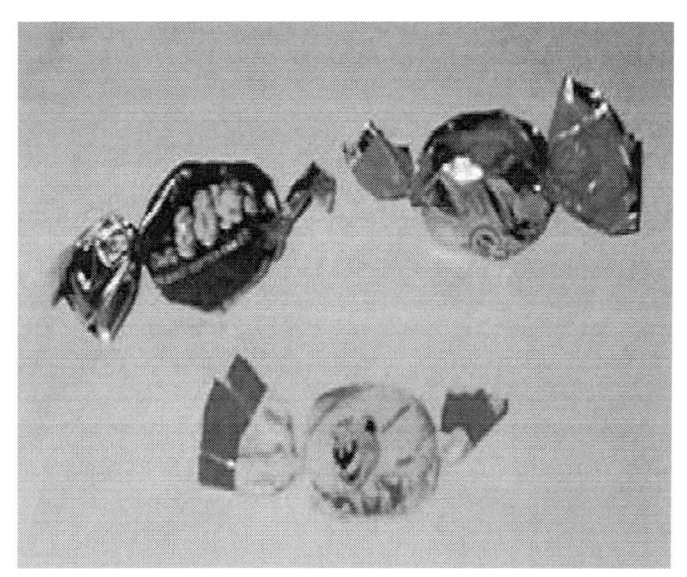

Candy from the set of *Per Manum*. Photo by Little Star.

"While waiting for the camera to move to a new position, Mitch asked me for a straw," remembers Little Star. "He then started shooting spitballs at the two crew guys who had sat down at the counter I was behind. He got off a couple of good shots before they too grabbed straws and started a full blown spitball war. Mitch even shot some at Kim Manners. Of course, Kim was outside so they just hit the glass wall. When Gillian started to walk in, Mitch turned to the crew guys and told them to get Gillian. Wisely, they didn't. We had quite some time to wait so Mitch sat down at the counter and started playing the IQ game. The two crew guys were also playing. No one had won yet so I had to throw out the challenge. I told them I have solved that game twice now. Then Mitch said he was playing for genius level. The variation of the game is to leave eight pegs in the board with no possible jumps. We worked on that together. First we figured out the only pattern that eight pegs could possibly be left in the board with no jumps possible. None of us solved that one. The most we ever left was six. One of the crew claimed he left seven, but no one actually saw it."

"They were finally ready to shoot that scene and since they could still see inside the Deli, I was told to wipe the counters," Little Star tells me. "Kim came in and told me exactly what area they could see and told me to stay within that area. That part of the counter has never been so clean! I might just be a blur in the background but I really doubt I'll be seen at all during that part."

"For the next scene, I was left alone in the Deli with one or two crew members scattered about," Little Star carries on. "They were filming outside. Here's the scene: Doggett gets in his truck, makes a U turn and drives away. Scully gets into her car which has the guest star of the week in the passenger seat, also makes a U turn and drives away. I sat down at a table by the window where I could see the monitors and the live action. Just on the other side of the glass was Kim Manners. I alternated between watching the monitors and the real people for a while, playing the IQ game and trying to watch Gillian inconspicuously. Finally I pulled out a book and read the whole thing. Yup, there is that much waiting around on the set. I read somewhere an actor saying, 'I act for free, I get paid to wait.' I don't know who said it but it's so true."

"Watching eventually got tiring so I curled up in a booth and tried to sleep," resumes Little Star. "That didn't last long. They were finally going to start shooting inside the Deli. Lisa came in, told me to get back behind the counter and told me what was going to happen. She showed me the script, said Robert will speak, Gillian will answer and that's when I walk up to them and set the coffee down in front of Robert. Then she handed me the sides of everything we were shooting that night plus the call sheet."

"First they shot with the cameras facing Mitch and Gillian," continues Little Star. "It ended up being very tight quarters. In order to get where I needed to be, they sandwiched me between the two cameras and directly behind me was the counter. They decided Robert needed to start from the same place. So here I am jammed into a tiny spot and then

Robert Patrick joins me. We shot Robert joining Gillian and Mitch, they spoke, and then I walked up to their table and set down the coffee. Wow, my big acting break! They all look at me then Robert says 'Thanks' I smiled and walked away. Well back to the small space between the two cameras. At one point, Robert and I were standing about two inches away from each other, facing each other and Robert said, 'Are you okay?' I answered, 'Yeah' but for some bizarre reason my voice was about two octaves too high."

"That's where I stood while they filmed the whole scene," picks up Little Star. "Gillian was right in my line of sight so I tried not to stare at her too much. I didn't want to make her nervous. While looking around, I noticed that Robert was wearing white boxers covered with dogs. I don't know if those were Robert's or if they were supposed to be Doggett's. The scene took place at 3:30 or so in the morning and Doggett was woken up and asked to come to the Deli and the script said he dressed in a hurry, which would probably explain why his boxers were visible in the first place."

"During the break while they moved the cameras, Gillian also noticed the boxers," Little Star goes on. "She asked what was on them so Robert pulled them out a little to show her the dogs. Gillian then called him 'Dog Butt' for a while. Gillian, Mitch, and Robert got along really well. They laughed and joked with each other in between takes. It was cool to see them laughing and giggling then get immediately serious when it was time to shoot. They teased each other too. They kept calling Robert "# 4', Mitch '# 3' and Gillian '# 2' according to their numbers on the call sheet. It was pretty funny and they all meant it in good fun. When they needed to move the cameras again they huddled together to do some game Gillian described for them. From what I could gather, they took turns writing something then they'd fold it down so the next person couldn't see it and they'd continue from there. I think they also took turns drawing parts of a picture. It took a while to do because they kept getting interrupted to shoot another take. Gillian started it, Robert took it next and Mitch finished it. While Mitch was finishing his turn Robert went out for a smoke. He told Gillian not to read it without him. Then they started getting silly, expressing how much he wanted to be there when they read/looked at it. When Mitch finished, they started yelling for # 4 so they could look at it. The three of them then huddled together in a booth and giggled like school kids."

"While they were doing this, most everyone else was playing the IQ game," Little Star tells me. "I finally solved it again and being the math teacher I am, I thought I'd figured out the sequence. So I tried it again and solved it again. One of the crew guys saw me solve it the second time and was impressed. I told him I'd figured it out and could solve it again and for some reason he didn't believe me. He bet me five bucks I couldn't do it again and by this time several crew members were watching us so I really had no choice but to bet him. I was a little nervous due to the crowd watching, but I solved it again and he forked over the five bucks. Another crew guy told me to try it starting with a different space open. I thought for a moment, trying to figure it out then asked if he wanted to bet me. He said no, but I solved it for him anyway."

"It got pretty boring after that," recounts Little Star. "I couldn't hear what Gillian, Mitch and Robert were laughing over; I had read my book and solved the game so I had nothing to do but wait. I listened to Kim Manners and someone else discussing directing and upcoming projects, etc. Someone came in and touched up my hair which was cool since they don't usually fuss with the extras."

"At 4:30 am they finally wrapped us," continues Little Star. "AD Bear said to say good-night to Gillian, Mitch, Robert and me. I followed them back to base camp, changed out of my waitressing outfit and looked for an opportunity to grab a picture with Gillian. Unfortunately, getting my voucher signed took longer than it should so all I could do was helplessly watch as Gillian walked by me, got into her car and drove away."

"All in all, it was an incredibly awesome experience," finishes Little Star. "I got home at 5 am, slept all the way till 6 am then got back up and headed to Los Angeles to teach middle school. The crew kept teasing me all night about having to work again so soon. I managed to stay awake all day and even lasted through Open House and having to deal with parents. By the time I got home at 8 pm however, I crashed. I slept very soundly till 6 am Friday morning. BTW, the hair people on X-Files are amazing. My hair stayed looking fabulous till I took it down Friday night. The other teachers said that for once I looked like a teacher and not one of the students."

8x09 Surekill

Written by: Greg Walker
Directed by: Terrence O'Hara
Summary: Agents Scully and Doggett are called in after several people have been killed from impossible locations. Scully suggests that the man they are looking for may have special seeing abilities. The investigation leads to a company run by twins, Dwight and Randall. One of them is legally blind and the other can see through walls.

AAA-1 Exterminators
1327 Palmetto St.
Los Angeles, Ca

8x10 Salvage

Written by: Jeffrey Bell
Directed by: Ron Hardy
Summary: Ray is out for revenge after being poisoned by an experimental metal made by Chamber Technologies. This smart metal is designed to be indestructible and turn electrical energy into mechanical energy. While working at a salvage yard, Ray comes across an illegally

dumped barrel containing the metal and slowly becomes more metallic and machine like.

St. Clare's Halfway House
Building 99
FOX Lot

8x11 The Gift

Written by: Frank Spotnitz
Directed by: Kim Manners
Summary: Doggett goes to Pennsylvania to interview Paul and Marie Hangemuhl after learning Mulder visited them there a week before he disappeared. Marie tells Doggett Mulder was inquiring about an Indian folk legend of a soul eater who can heal the sick. When Doggett finds the creature, he tries to leave town with it, but is shot and killed by the Sherriff. The creature consumes Doggett, absorbing his death and thus finally becoming free.

Soul Eater Residence
Ventura Farms
235 W. Potrero Ave.
Thousand Oaks, Ca

8x12 Badlaa

Written by: John Shiban
Directed by: Tony Wharmby
Summary: A legless beggar attacks a man in an Indian airport bathroom and the next day the man is found dead in his hotel room in Washington D.C. Scully examines the body and finds that the man was dead before he left India and suggests something entered him to use him as a way to travel. FBI Associate Chuck Burks theorizes it may have been a Siddhi mystic, an Indian man capable of clouding reality. The beggar

can become invisible and can become anyone he wishes. He is finally shot by Scully who finds the man disguised as a young boy in a school.

Suhar International Airport
Cruise Ship Terminals
Queens Hwy
Long Beach, Ca

"My friends and I arrived at the location of filming around 3 pm," fan Tiffany Robinson tells me after her visit to the private residence used for Quentin and Trevor's homes. "Director of Photography Bill Roe came over and asked us if we were X-Files fans and we enthusiastically said yes. He then said that Robert and Gillian would not be there until about 7 pm. He was really nice, and we were so grateful he told us that information."

"Our group [returned] to stand around and Paul Harrison, the key assistant location manager, came over and talked to us," continues Tiffany. "He was talking about the neighborhood and saying how nice it was. He also told us that they spend $10,000 every 5 minutes filming!"

"About 20 minutes after [most of] the other fans left, we saw Gillian Anderson, and some other people, walking out," carries on Tiffany. "We were waving but she didn't seem to see us. She wrapped her coat around her tightly and she bounced over to get into her SUV. As her SUV was pulling out of the driveway, we were still waving at her. Before it left, she rolled the window down and she yelled out, 'I'll stop by later!"

"Not 5 minutes after she left, we saw Robert Patrick come out from where they had been filming. We began to wave at him, too, but he wasn't looking over at us, either," Tiffany excitedly explains. "He put some things in a van parked on the side of the street, and then to our complete surprise and happiness he started walking across the street to us!"

"He shook my hand first, and then everyone else's too," exclaims Tiffany. "Then I, being the complete nut that I am, proceeded to profess my love for him and his character Agent Doggett. I told him I completely adored Doggett, and thought he was so awesome playing the character. Everyone else chimed in too. Robert said to us, 'You know, I'm really happy to hear that because I thought that, you know, the fans wouldn't accept Doggett.' Then he asked us if we had stuff for him to sign or anything. I handed him the *Entertainment Weekly* magazine with him and Gillian on the front, and he began signing his name. My friend Kate asked him if he knew why Scully's pregnancy wasn't showing yet, and he chuckled a bit and said slyly, 'I don't know, you'll just have to keep watching.' Someone then asked if we could take pictures with him. He said it was okay. Robert was so incredibly generous with his time, and so wonderful. It was so nice of him to hang out with us and take pictures and sign things so generously on his break from filming that evening."

"About half an hour after we met Robert, we saw Gillian's SUV pull up in the driveway across the street," recalls Tiffany. "She got out of the vehicle, and then she started to cross the street to come over to us. While she was signing, Kate asked her why Scully is not showing yet. Gillian totally laughed and she said, 'Don't fucking ask me!' Gillian said she was trying to put it off as long as possible. Bill Roe came back over then. Gillian turned around and said, 'Uh-oh, it's the big boss man!' She asked him cutely, 'Are you going to kill me?' Gillian finished signing our stuff, and as she left, we thanked her profusely. It was one of the best nights ever, and I'll never forget it."

8x13 Medusa

Written by: Frank Spotnitz
Directed by: Richard Compton
Summary: Agents Scully and Doggett have a 5 hour time limit to solve a case in a subway tunnel. Doggett and a team go into the tunnel to investigate and find a glowing gooey liquid. Scully informs Doggett that the glowing substance is seawater with a small creature living in it which

she suggests is triggered by sweat. Doggett wets his gun with the goo and throws it onto the tracks as the train comes which electrocutes the water and kills the creature.

8x14 This Is Not Happening

Written by: Chris Carter & Frank Spotnitz
Directed by: Kim Manners
Summary: Abductees being left for dead in a field by aliens are picked up by Jeremiah Smith and Absalom who then heal them. Meanwhile, in an attempt to get more ideas to find Mulder, Doggett introduces Scully and Skinner to Monica Reyes, an agent who specializes in ritualistic crimes. The four follow a lead to the camp where the two men treat the returned abductees. Agent Mulder is found dead and Scully rushes back to get help from Jeremiah Smith only to find he has been abducted himself.

Scully and Skinner Motel
La Cresenta Motel
2413 Foothill Blvd.
Glendale, Ca
***This site was also used in *Sein Und Zein* and *The Truth II*

Absalom Abductees Cabins
Melody Ranch Motion Picture Studio
24715 Oak Creek Ave.,
Newhall, Ca

"I shot the episode *"This is Not Happening"* on Friday, January 12, 2001," Patricia Steffy tells me. "It wasn't my first episode with Kim Manners, but it was perhaps one of the most memorable, but for an unexpected reason. Kim's birthday was over the weekend, but the cast and crew decided to throw him a surprise party. Because I was already on set, I wandered over when I started hearing the applause and cheers.

I'll never forget hearing Kim address the crowd of well-wishers. The depth of feeling and connection he had with those people was obvious. He talked about how eight seasons might seem like a long time, but he would be happy if they could have another eight together because he loved every minute of working with them all. I remember looking at this gigantic poster board of pictures that everyone had signed with colorful messages for him."

"As he was leaving the party—we had another 10 hours of shooting—I wished him a happy birthday," continues Patricia. "He stopped and had a conversation with me. The conversation itself was mostly about whether or not I had worked the show before, if I was having fun, was I an actor, etc—nothing earth-shattering in content. Now, I don't know how many people know about the process of being an extra, but it's extremely rare when any director will actually take the time to talk to you, let alone someone as prolific and revered as Kim Manners. The entire time we talked, I kept thinking, *"Don't you know who you are?"* That's just the kind of man Kim was: a person of amazing energy who wanted to know about the people around him—even if they were lowly extras."

"Random aside, I fell asleep waiting to shoot and woke up under the spaceship lights of the ship that had abducted Mulder," concludes Patricia. "Yeah, strange doesn't begin to cover it."

8x18 Three Words

Written by: Chris Carter & Frank Spotnitz
Directed by: Tony Wharmby
Summary: After a news report of a man who was shot and killed as he ran to the White House, Mulder believes the man had information about a coming alien invasion. Absalom kidnaps Doggett to get information from a government building, but is shot and killed before he reaches the information. After hearing about this, Mulder enlists the Gunmen to help

him find the evidence Absalom was looking for by breaking into a government building.

Cheviot Hills Park
2551 Motor Ave.
Los Angeles, Ca
***This location was also in *Lord of the Flies* and *The Unnatural*
White House
727 Kenneth Rd.
Glendale, Ca

Federal Statistics Center
LA Center Studios
1202 W. 5th St.
Los Angeles, Ca
***Also used to play Federal Building in *Fight the Future*

"For whatever reason, before I was even writing music, there was some part in my character related to sadness in a dramatic way," says Mark Snow when I asked him about the reunion scene in the hospital in *Three Words*. "You were so used to seeing Mulder as Joe Friday so to speak - no affect; just the facts ma'am. That was the beauty of the marriage between these characters because he was not impressed with things, so to speak, and then these moments where he would let it all hang out emotionally that always got to me. Before *The X-Files*, I was known as The Comedy Guy or the Romantic Guy. When those emotional moments came, like when Mulder wakes up from his coma; I just loved to write melodic music, with real depth and heart. And to see David get emotional, well, that wasn't what he did every week. It was on special occasions like this, and it impressed me how well he did it and how much I embraced it and made it so memorable for me."

"Some of the challenges we faced in Los Angeles were when we had to hang from these harnesses and do sneaky stuff as The Lone

Gunmen in *Three Words*," recalls Tom Braidwood. "That was probably the hardest stuff to do for me because that kind of thing is really uncomfortable. It was a long day for me; I probably wore that harness for close to five or six hours. It was multiple takes, where we could be lowered down to rest, but we kept the harness on because it was a lot of work to take it off and then put it back on again properly. It was pretty brutal really tiring by the end. On the plus side, it was funny when Frohike goes to give Mulder a hug after he returns from the dead. David ad libbed the line about my hands on his ass, and I think I accidentally did touch his ass. We laughed quite a bit after that."

"Well for Tom, I think was painful because they don't make harnesses that small, so it wasn't a great fit where you needed it the most, if you catch my drift," shares Dean Haglund. "For me, I really liked it, because it was fun repelling and hanging around and listening to the director through a loud speaker, if I remember correctly."

"I'm embarrassed about *Three Words* because the harness was so uncomfortable on my nether regions that I found it hard to breathe," adds Bruce Harwood. "The crew took me down and left me out of a lot of the shots. Some of the shots I was sitting on a stepladder while Tom and Dean hung above me. Looking back, I wonder if I wasn't being a wuss, since Tom and Dean didn't complain at all."

"I was an extra in the teaser scene outside of the White House," Adrienne Doucette tells me. "I was a tourist and someone watching the action as this guy jumps the fence and runs towards the White House, which is a replica in Glendale. It's actually a library and a beautiful building that looks just like the White House. On set, I saw one of our friends, Chris, who had gotten a job with the show as a stand-in for Nicholas Lea and Robert Patrick because he was the perfect height. It's a small world."

8x16 Vienen

Written by: Steve Maeda
Directed by: Ron Hardy
Summary: After one worker dies of severe flash burns on an oil rig, Mulder believes it is due to the black oil. Agents Mulder and Doggett quarantine the rig and Mulder hypothesizes that the oil rig is drilling infected oil. The two agents learn that everyone on the rig is infected with the black oil except the worker who was killed because he was born with an immunity to it. After getting off the oil rig before it bursts into flames and returning to D.C., Mulder gets fired from the FBI leaving Doggett in charge of the X-files.

Galpex-Orpheus Platform
Oil Rig
Santa Barbara, Ca

Oil Tanks
CENCO Refining Company
12345 Lakeland Rd.
Santa Fee Springs, Ca

Getting out to the off shore oil rig from land proved to be quite an experience for many of the crew members. "It took a long time to get set up over there, which is why we pre-loaded everything on the boat," recalls Mac Gordon. "The boat ride was about 30 minutes. We had safety guys, Coast Guard guys, oil guys, just all kinds of people out there with us. In my opinion, it was one of the better looking episodes. We loaded up via crane and brought supplies to the people that were on the rig. You had to leave the crew boat to get onto the lower level platform and then walk up many stairs. You had to use a rope swing and that was amazing to see Michelle MacLaren, the co-executive producer, and the hair and make-up people swing over and let go at the appropriate time, otherwise they swing back onto the boat and then we'd have to send them back over."

"One of my favorite stories on that show was *Vienen*, which took place on an off shore oil rig and at the end of it, we blew it up," shares Michelle MacLaren. "The locations team found a shut down factory that looked like an oil rig for the exterior shots that allowed us to blow up. We built the interior on stage and then we shot for a couple of days on an actual off shore oil rig and that was very cool. Getting off the rig was an experience also. Since the oil rigs are off shore, a boat came to pick us up, and took us to and from the rig, going through these huge swells. Because of these swells, there was a Tarzan swing, where you had to grab the rope as the boat came to the tip of the swell and they said 'Jump!' and you can leap onto the boat from the rig. There was a 'Catcher' on the boat in case you missed your mark. Well, these are pretty hard core oil guys, and getting onto the rig was no problem for me, but getting off was. These are pretty hard core oil rig guys and when I used the Tarzan swing to get off the rig, my timing was off and I missed the mark. The Catcher caught me by my ankles mid air and I had to slide down his body to get onto the boat. They were all laughing pretty hard. This is not an exciting story, but I have to say it was pretty scary and I was a little bit intimidated by the size of the waves and the swells. *The X-Files* was big and challenging, but it was exciting and I was very fortunate to have been a part of it."

"I'm not great with heights, but I went up on the helideck, which is about a hundred and fifty feet above the water, and all of a sudden I got a sense of vertigo so I slammed myself onto the helideck and had to be tossed down by Cory Kaplan," laughs Ilt Jones.

"This was a fun and interesting challenge for me and we got yelled out by the coastal commission," continues Ilt. "They said our helicopters and crew woke up the sea lions that were sleeping on the beach. In actual fact, the crew that was hanging around base camp, near the supposed awake sea lions, reported that the sea lions were snoring loudly throughout the whole proceeding. They were snoring so loudly in fact that you could barely hear the roar of the helicopters."

8x19 Alone

Written by: Frank Spotnitz
Directed by: Frank Spotnitz
Summary: Scully goes on maternity leave and Agent Leyla Harrison accompanies Doggett on his investigation of a missing caretaker. Harrison is attacked and dragged away by a monster, then Doggett goes missing after falling into a trap. While staking out Mr. Stites's property, Mulder sees the reptile and chases it until it goes inside the house. He tries to warn Mr. Stite's of the reptile in his house only to find Mr. Stites's is the monster.

Elderly Man's House
Rocky's Jumbo Burgers
12653 Osbourne St.
Pacoima, Ca

"I had the honor and privilege to meet Kim Manners in 2001 on *The X-Files* sound stage at Fox Studios," fan Janet Shull tells me. "My daughter and I were guests of Gillian, and were chaperoning a girl that had won a raffle prize - a day on the set - at a Neurofibromatosis benefit that was held the previous December."

"The filming that we saw was *Alone*, and was directed by Frank Spotnitz," she continues. "We were allowed to bring a certain number of items for Gillian to sign, and for some reason, I had the *Humbug* script with me. Frank signed it for me, then to our surprise, Kim walked in, and it was a 'pinch me' moment. He couldn't have been sweeter or more accessible. I showed him the script, and he said, 'Oh, Humbug!' He signed it, 'Trust No One' - Kim Manners. What a thrill for us! We were truly lucky, as David Duchovny was also there. He was barely around that season, but that day he had scenes with Gillian, and we were there. Téa also showed up with West. We were seated in director's chairs directly behind Frank, and right next to David and Gillian's chair. Talk about a memory to last a lifetime."

8x20 Essence

Written by: Chris Carter
Directed by: Kim Manners
Summary: Following a news report on the destruction of Zeus Genetics, Mulder and Doggett go to Dr. Parenti's office and discover many deformed babies making Mulder wonder about Scully's pregnancy. Mrs. Scully hires a baby nurse to help her daughter around the house. After Mulder tells Scully someone is monitoring her pregnancy, she finds the nurse switching her pills. Mulder has Agent Reyes take Scully away to a safer location out of state.

FBI Building
3700 Wilshire Blvd.
Los Angeles, Ca

"We had spoken to Kim on the set of *Existence* and he told us if we wanted to see something really cool on Friday night, they were going to be filming a big stunt and we're gonna want to see it," Kathleen Keegan tells me. "He told us that David would not be there, but Mitch would, and we should come anyway. It turned out to be the scene where Billy Miles jumps off of the FBI building into the garbage truck. They filmed it in two different locations. The actual jump, with a stunt double landing on a giant inflatable mattress, was on Wilshire Blvd. in downtown Los Angeles. Zachary Ansley, who played Billy Miles, was there but we didn't get a chance to talk to him since they were really busy. They filmed Zach up on the roof, and then the stunt double falling. The second location is near the Staples Center and they had blocked off 6th to 8th St.

This was filmed from the prospective of being on the parking structure and seeing Billy Miles in the garbage truck. I'm not sure why, but both Mitch and his wife Arlene were there. When we showed up, Kim was really excited to see us. He was bubbly and full of energy. We also saw them film in the parking structure on West Century Park for at least two weeks. They were filming on the first floor of the structure, but they had blocked off the first three floors. The street the parking structure is on is quite long and a sort of an incline. We were there on the day that Skinner shot Krycek. When Kim called for that scene via walkie talkie from the parking structure, people were humming the *'Dead Man Walking'* tune down the street. As we were walking around, exploring the area, we passed by some cast trailers since they were spread out along the street. We walked past the trailers and we hear the door open and then someone starts walking directly behind us. My friend and I kept talking, not paying attention and then that person is walking so fast they are barreling down on us. I moved to the side to let the person pass. When the person doesn't pass us, I look behind me and I see Nic Lea, laughing his ass off since he scared us. Someone had an old Ford pick-up truck and at one point Robert Patrick was tinkering with the engine, dressed in his FBI suit. It was common for crew to use scooters and bicycles on the lot and set, which is why David bought the crew Razor scooters for the end of the year gift. One of the Productions Assistant's (PA's) had received an old fashioned scooter for his birthday the week before. It was red and silver, kind of like the Radio Flyer. Everyone loved the PA's scooter so much, that whenever the poor kid turned his back, somebody was off riding his brand new scooter. As we're sitting on the sidewalk near base camp, we see Robert flying down the hill on the scooter with this big, shit eating grin on his face. His FBI suit jacket is unbuttoned and flying in the breeze behind him. It was the funniest picture. Everyone starts cracking up; he was having a good old time. At the end of the night, we made sure to thank him for inviting us and tell him that we had a great time. This was also not a great neighborhood to be in at night, so we thanked the crew for keeping an eye on us and made sure we were safe."

8x21 Existence

Written by: Chris Carter
Directed by: Kim Manners
Summary: Reyes takes Scully to Georgia to have her baby. Doggett and Mulder become suspicious of Kersh after they learn of his late night meetings with intelligence officer Knowle Rohrer. Billy Miles shows up in Georgia along with several other super soldiers to see the baby's birth. Scully gives birth to a baby boy who she names William.

Democrat Hot Springs
Paramount Ranch
2903 Cornell Rd.
Agoura Hills, Ca

"I was back in the LA area, driving with some friends from Malibu to the outlets up in Camarillo on one of the canyon roads," recounts Kathleen Keegan. "We were almost at the freeway and I see this florescent pink sign that reads *Existence* with an arrow pointing to the right. Without knowing for sure if this was *The X-Files*, we followed the arrow to Paramount Ranch, which was the same set they used for *Dr. Quinn, Medicine Woman*, for all those years. They had filmed the birth earlier that day before we arrived, Gillian had just left for the day, but Annabeth was there, finishing up from the birth scene, and getting ready to leave. This was also the first time I had met Harry Bring. I knew his name from the credits and I knew he was a big producer guy. Harry is a practical joker. The crew was trying to prepare us for him because they knew he was gonna drive us crazy with his jokes. The next thing we know, this goofball comes over to us with fun glasses, fake teeth and he starts to chase us around with a whoopee cushion. It was so funny because he's supposed to be the big boss! We talked to Kevin Cooper, David's assistant, that day and we found out that David would be arriving back from New York that night to film the helicopter scenes. Since Paramount Ranch is a park, it closes after dark, and we were told that we would not be allowed to see the night scenes because of the danger and liability."

William's birthplace. Photo by Erica Fraga

Season Nine: Believe in the Future

Season 9 signified the end of one of the best television shows in history. The cast and crew also have their own favorite episodes that they either worked on or watched. Actress Annabeth Gish reveals what it was like joining the cast and doing her own stunts on *Aubrey Pauley*. "Gillian is a formidable presence," replies Annabeth. "She is strong and extremely smart, just like Scully. She is also very warm and very funny. She was kind to me the entire way through my X-Files experience. I admire her greatly and we all laughed a lot! There was great humor on the show and it was always easy and wonderful to laugh. Gillian especially could get very silly - which is the best trait for anyone to have in this business where people tend to take themselves so super seriously. David is great. He's another whip-smart actor with an impressive presence. One of my favorite episodes to film was *Audrey Pauley*. Kim and I had such fun meandering through those hospital scenes and the otherworldly death-scape that was Reyes' journey for the episode. It was also in *Audrey Pauley* that I got to do the biggest stunt of my career: a jump from a 30 ft. descender. It was exciting to take such a huge leap off the stage onto the mats--feeling the pride and exhilaration that came with it. I felt safe with Kim and the stunt team and felt proud of both the emotional and physical work on that episode."

"I will never forget Kim Manners and he will surely last in my memory as an example of a director and a man second to none," concludes Annabeth.

"There is a lot of visual effects in this particular episode we're doing, so sometimes if I have time I'll storyboard what I want," Kim tells Matt Hurwitz about his time on *Audrey Pauley*. "And otherwise we'll just sit down, have a closed door visual effects meeting. And I'll visualize my scenes and tell them here's what I want to do and how I want to do it. If we run up against a wall, we'll involve Frank and/or Chris. And then the effects are budgeted, they bring me the budget, and then we start compromising. What can we live without, what can we do differently? And we come up with other solutions. For instance, in this one, we had

Tracy Ellis's character, Audrey disappear on camera. Well, we had a hundred forty some odd thousand dollar visual effects budget, so we found another way to do that. We play a two-shot at some point in the scene, so we tie the two actresses together, let's say Annabeth and Tracy and then you gut to Annabeth and in her face there's an 'oh shit' reaction, and then [an arm?] straight up on a crane, all right, and see that she's completely alone. So there are other creative ways to trim budget. You find yourself doing that, especially in this medium."

Improbable allowed series creator Chris Carter to get behind the camera again and direct his last episode of the series. Chris shares his motivation and purpose for this quirky episode.

"Mark did music for *Improbable*, but I think he worked around the music from the French entertainer, Karl Zero," Chris tells me. "I had heard his music and it was so far out and it fit with exactly what I wanted to do because I wanted to recreate Little Italy and they had not had their yearly celebration that year because of September 11. I wanted to create that festival. It's an interesting episode."

Scary Monsters signified the return of fan inspired character Leyla Harrison, the shy young accountant from Season 8 *Alone* who followed the adventures of Mulder and Scully as close as any television viewer.

"The inspiration for this episode was basically panic," writer Tom Schnauz says of *Scary Monsters*. "We needed to get the script done, and I pretty much had the Teaser locked in. I even remember when I pitched it. I said I was embarrassed over how basic it was: kid scared of what's beneath his bed, but the twist being his Dad keeps him locked in the room with the monster. I had a whole other story that wasn't working, and in an effort to move forward, breaking the story as a group with the producers, I believe it was Vince who hit on the idea of the boy as the cause of everything bad. We tried to keep it away from *Twilight Zone* kid-in-the-cornfield by making him unable to control what he was doing, but as the cards went on the board, we realized we needed a villain, and it was the boy."

"Frank pitched early on in the process that Leyla Harrison be in the episode," continues Tom. "It was a funny way to comment on the pro-Mulder/anti-Doggett members of the audience. She was so annoying to Doggett! I really wanted to make this a Doggett episode because there were so many before this where he, as a non-believer, was essentially wrong about what was happening. I wanted him to be the hero. And in the end, Leyla saw that."

"In a scene near the end, Leyla Harrison and Gabe Rotter were supposed to walk out hand-in-hand together," concludes Tom. "Well, I heard Kim saw it in the editing room and said, 'When did this turn into the fucking Brady Bunch!' I laughed when I heard it, and luckily Frank Spotnitz found an artful way to cut that moment out. What I was originally nervous about, that big personality and impressively foul vocabulary, is exactly what I miss about Kim. I learned so much in the brief time I knew him."

"*Scary Monsters* was a case both of wanting to honor Leyla again and bring back Jolie Jenkins, who'd done such a great job for us the season before," explains Frank. "As I recall, Tom Schnauz's original story called for another FBI agent, and it seemed natural to make it Agent Harrison again."

Controversial episode, *Jump the Shark* crossed over the worlds of *The X-Files* and *The Lone Gunmen*. Having *The Lone Gunmen* grace our television screens meant moments full of humor for the fans and quotable one liners from Melvin Frohike. The departure of The Lone Gunmen from the show, however, left many fans angry, confused, or just plain in denial about their death. Writer Frank Spotnitz talked about why he pushed the studio to get the episode made the way they wanted.

"This episode almost never was because there was zero support for doing it," Frank brings to light. "The studio was hostile to the idea and it was a constant fight to get the money and negotiate with the actors because they did not want to do it. We were determined, since this was the last year of *The X-Files,* that we were going to have our farewell with these characters. When we finally decided that this would be their death, it became a much stronger argument with the studio. It's a miracle that we pulled it off."

"I can't say I regret killing them because, as you know, no one ever really dies in *The X-Files*," Frank shares with me. "I thought then and now that it was right to give those characters a big send-off before the series went off the air. But I do feel tonally it was a mistake to end the episode on such a somber note. I wish we'd ended on a laugh or smile."

"I can't recall exactly how I got the news, but I think Frank phoned me to tell me," adds Bruce Harwood. "Killing us off didn't really surprise me, though. After nine years, I think we did all we were ever going to do. The only thing I wish was that the Gunmen had died in a huge explosion. For example, a situation where there is a ticking time bomb. We send Mulder and Scully to safety claiming we can defuse it, then the three of us settle down to work. Time then runs out, and a big fiery explosion that takes down an entire building, our faces superimposed over the flames with sad music playing. That would have been cool, though I understand why Frank, Vince and John went the way they did."

"As for convincing the studio to kill us off, the studio hated our characters after the cancellation of *The Lone Gunmen,* and told Frank that he could not bring our characters back to the ninth season at all," continues Bruce. "Frank had to convince them to bring us back! I think if the studio objected to anything, it was wasting time on our characters long enough to kill us off."

"I personally liked the way we were sent off," shares Dean Haglund. "I remember I got a call while I was out biking on a gorgeous day on the beach. Frank said he was killing us off in a cool way and not to worry. I was quite pleased about that, because I thought they either were just not going just not mentioned it, or send us off into the sunset with a hobo bag on a stick. I remember after it aired I got a call from the Ramones saying they all cried at the end of that episode, which is not how I think of them, really. I think someone sent a pig to the production office in Los Angeles to protest the canceling of *The Lone Gunmen,* but I don't think that helped since it went to head of programming, who never saw it."

Writer Tom Schnauz makes a rare appearance in this episode, as a speaker at the conference. I asked him about his experience being in front of the camera and whose idea it was.

"I seem to remember it being Frank," replies Tom. "I *think* it was his idea, because no one actually asked me. I tend to blame Frank because he also threw me into a *Night Stalker* episode. We needed a neighbor character, and right away Frank said, 'Tom will do it.' I remember walking across the FOX lot and bumping into Tim Silver, and he said, 'I hear you're the scientist.' And I laughed. It was one of those fake laughs, because I thought he was making a joke that I didn't get. But as we kept talking, I finally had to say, 'What are you talking about?' Then he explained that yes, 'you will be on camera.' I'm pretty much game for anything, so I wrote a very silly, filthy speech, and showed it to Frank. I remember Frank handing the speech back to me across his desk, and all he said was, 'Go with God.'"

Season nine was full of emotional roller coasters for the viewers. David Duchovny came back in season nine to direct and co-write *William*, the show where a supposedly barren Scully gives up her miracle child for adoption. "Working so much with Rob and Kim has influenced my directing in that they are really strong action directors and they know where to place the camera, and know how to tell the action story of the show with a camera," says David Duchovny. "Kim loved creepy, low angles. Personally I don't like to have the camera go up my nose, but it can give you a creepy point of view for sure. And he did that a lot. Chris would have influenced my story telling as a writer, I don't know how he did, it just would have happened over the years. The blessing about doing a show is that you have your head down and you do the work. You never think that anything is more important than anything else. No scene feels more important than the other and *William* was no different than any other episode I would have acted in. It had emotional beats and it had a story. I think it was important for Gillian to show that she was torn and to somehow show a *Sophie's Choice* that she would have to make to save the child, to make it better for him."

After nine seasons, trying to keep the show fresh and engaging was paramount to any of the writers. "I think the thing you struggle with is that, in particular with the mythology, you don't know when the story is going to end," explains Chris Carter. "Many shows end after a season, sometimes shorter, but we knew we were going longer than that, but we didn't know that we were going longer than five. I think one of the things that we worked the hardest on, and I'd say we struggled with, was keeping the mythology fresh through those times."

"Working on a demanding show like *The X-Files* can take its physical toll on a person. "I kept at it pretty regularly for the entire nine seasons," Chris continues. "All I can say is on the last season of the show, I was writing or re-writing a lot and I would take a nap every day. As the season went on, it became two naps a day. Those nine years caught up with me pretty fast."

Executive Producer and writer Frank Spotnitz was able to direct one last time before the series ended in 2002. "I think I put a lot of pressure on myself when I was writing episodes that I knew I would direct," says Frank of his episode *Daemonicus*. "It was a standalone, but I wanted it to be special in some way. *Daemonicus* presented an opportunity to get new insight into Doggett's feelings for Scully. I have to say, I had a great time making this episode."

I asked Frank about the repulsive vomit scene in the mental hospital. "There actually was a tube that delivered the vomit up the side of the actor's face - we simply removed it digitally afterward. I actually hadn't intended for the vomiting to go on for so long, but after I saw it in the editor's cut, the outrageousness of it appealed to me and so we kept it long."

"A great lesson I learned from Frank Spotnitz is it's not what you show; it's what you don't show," Dan Sackheim informs me of Frank's influence. "It's far more compelling to tease the audience and leave them wanting more. Unfortunately with *The Host*, I don't think I left anything to the imagination. It was just a guy in a rubber suit. I would do that episode completely different."

Release allowed the paternal side of Agent Doggett's character to be revealed, as he laid his son's memory to rest. "It was a difficult scene, but Kim was there to guide us along," says Robert. "I can think of no worst nightmare for a parent than to lose their child."

When Robert Patrick was asked if there was anything he would have liked to have seen with his character if the show had continued into a 10th year, he replied, "I think Doggett was very attracted to Reyes and was probably working on having a relationship with her if we had had more time, but we ran out of shows," he replies. "I would have liked to see the relationship with Reyes explored more."

"I always saw Doggett as a guy you could depend on to do the right thing when it needed to be done; a man that understood that character is how and what you do when no one is watching," replies Robert Patrick when I asked him how he would describe his character. "I think he would have done anything for Scully and the same for Reyes."

"I loved every minute of working on *The X-Files*," reports Robert Patrick. "The hardest thing I had to deal with was letting go when we stopped. I loved showing up every day to work. I am sure I complained here and there, but I truly enjoyed the experience and the fans."

When Annabeth Gish was asked where she saw her character in the future, had the series not ended. "I always felt and played a great, but buried love between Doggett and Reyes," she replies. "I'm not sure if that is what Chris and Frank built into their back-story, but for me, Reyes was always in a kind of love with him; there were just too many layers to get through to open his heart. As an actress that is the best tension to play--unrequited love; a love that can never be fulfilled. It keeps you wanting; desiring; hoping as a character in every scene.

For actor Jeff Gulka, *The X-Files* was a multitude of learning experiences. "Working on the show was quite interesting, because when I was little everyone would treat me like a little kid and they would always talk about their vulgar jokes and I really didn't understand it, but by the end of it, I was about fifteen I was getting it and people were a lot more comfortable around me I think," reveals Jeff Gulka.

"Three years later after doing *Dreamland*, I get a call from my agent and he tells me I've been invited back to *The X-Files*," reports Julia Vera. "In my mind I thought they were having a party. I went down to 20th century FOX to play another Indian Woman for the series finale and the cast and crew start greeting me with so much warmth love. I'm overwhelmed with all this attention. I was really taken aback with the wonderful enthusiasm. It was just an amazing experience and I will love it for the rest of my life. I was a fan of *The X-Files* from the very beginning. I was so happy to be on this wonderful show. My greatest experience was *The X-Files*."

Scientific details on the show were never overlooked by the crew. The show had such an academic following that one lucky fan was able to act as a consultant on the show. "One of the X-Philes Anonymous (XPA) members, who is now a pediatrician in San Diego, used to write a critique of the medical terminology used in that week's episode and it got the attention of FOX," says Kathleen Keegan. "FOX asked her if she would do medical consulting on the scripts, working with their researcher, Katrina Cabrera, but she went un-credited and did not get paid. She did it out of pure love for the show. FOX would courier the scripts to her at least a month in advance, read it, make notes, and send it back. About once a month she would drive up to Los Angeles and have meetings with 1013. They would debate back and forth and ask her opinion on things."

The cast and crew were lucky enough to have nine seasons full of memories and crazy moments. "One day Kim mentioned how in high school it became a kind of code that all the 'loose girls' wore red and black on Fridays," continues Nina. "Immediately most of the women on set collaborated to have a Red and Black Friday, but did not tell Kim. I picked a Friday and I made sure all the women knew to prepare. It took Kim a couple of hours, since we all did not walk on to the set at once. After an hour or two, Kim looks up and gets the 'wait a second' look on his face and says something like, 'Is it slut Friday?'

"The craziest thing I ever did was let Gillian drive a car with 2 cameras attached to the outside of it," recalls Tom Braidwood. "She was a great driver, but she never enjoyed doing that because she was nervous and uncomfortable being responsible for these cameras worth thousands of dollars. I hated it when we had to do that kind of stuff because she gets worried. In fact there was a scene, I forget the show's name, where a taxi was roaring up to a motel and Gillian jumps out of the back seat. Well, what they had done was make up a taxi from an old police car and unbeknownst to her and anyone else, the car doors would not open from the inside and she could not get out. It was the whole elaborate set up and then she could not get out of the car. It was pretty funny."

"The locations that we had to shoot in for the show were often pretty dirty" recalls Nina Jack. "I often wondered if I was the only one who went home at night and had to scrub the grime off my hands and grit off my teeth." Hence the following call sheet musing: Can someone please explain to me why alien activity only happens in cold forests and in hot, sweaty deserts? Why don't they ever visit tropical paradises, like Hawaii or Fiji, where Mulder and Scully have to search on gorgeous white sand beaches and lush, flowery landscapes in year round 75 degree weather? Just wondering."

"The easiest thing for me to do on location or set was initial contact with location personnel or landlords," replies Harry Bring when I ask him about finding locations for the show. "The general response was, 'Oh my god, you're from *The X-Files*? Come in and have a cup of coffee!' We were always well received, from the following. There were plenty of people that had never seen the show, but they knew about it. The door was always open because we had such a good reputation."

"The finale was the first episode we had chartered helicopters," continues Harry. "In movies we had done this, but never when I was a producer or a UPM, or even an assistant director. In features, you have enough money and a time element to fly your crew in and out of locations and to do so, on a television show, was unheard of. But we did it for both our scouting and shooting, because we had to get up to Fresno and back to Borrego Springs all in one day."

A view of the man made Indian stricter in Anza Borrego. (Photo by Harry Bring)

"I was doing the gag real for the finale of the series," remembers Paul Rabwin. "Harry Bring and I had concocted a plan where we had this beautiful camera move with Mark Snow's music in the basement office. I was behind the desk and I gave this impassioned little speech about how wonderful *The X-Files* had been over the years and this was our final gag real. I knew it was not going to be funny because it was a solemn momentous occasion. At that point, Harry Bring appears and puts a huge pie right in my face. I wipe my eyes off, go over to Harry who has his buck teeth in and tells me 'I don't think so.' I thought it was the silliest thing to take a pie in the face."

The Truth was the end of *The X-Files* on television. The cast and crew gave it their best, while Kim directed his heart out for his 53rd episode. "*The Truths I and II* were very special episodes because it was the grand finale; the final bow," declares Laurie Holden. "And everyone that had been on the series for years, part of the conspiracy if you will, showed up to pay tribute and honor this last and final chapter. Many of us had moved on to other shows, or were shooting movies, but we all flew in and gathered to participate in this incredible storytelling; to send the show out in style, with a real bang. It was a real testament to the quality of the show, to Chris Carter, and to our amazing cast and crew. It was an honor to be a part of something so special."

Season Nine

Filming Locations

9x01 Nothing Important Happened Today

Written by: Chris Carter & Frank Spotnitz
Directed by: Kim Manners
Summary: Doggett begins his investigation of Kersh only to have Mulder disappear again. Reyes and Doggett are also investigating the deaths of an environmental protection agent and a water reclamation plant worker. While searching the plant, Skinner and Doggett find many files about chloramine, a drug the government added to the water supply.

Dean Haglund had to done more than a Ramones T-Shirt and glasses for this episode. In a cross over episode with The Lone Gunmen, the same blue faced Langly *from All About Yves* makes an appearance at Agent Doggett's doorstep. I asked Dean about this paint experience. "It wasn't too bad, and it matched my eyes," replies Dean. "Plus it made my teeth look whiter. The hard part is removing it afterwards, particularly from that dimple in my chin. I think that is why I never auditioned for the Blue Man Group show in Vegas."

9x02 Nothing Important Happened Today II

Written by: Chris Carter & Frank Spotnitz
Directed by: Tony Wharmby
Summary: Shannon McMahon informs Doggett, Reyes, and Scully that the government is putting chloramine in the water supply to breed a generation of super soldiers, such as herself. Scully learns that there is something special about William. Reyes gets information about a naval ship that is conducting experiments that might relate to Scully and her child, but before the agents came have a thorough look around, the ship explodes.

Medical Ship (U.S.S. Valor)
U.S.S. Lane Victory
Long Beach, Ca

Casey's Bar
613 S. Grand Ave.
Los Angeles, Ca
***Played as Mulder's bar in *Fight the Future*

9x03 Daemonicus

Written by: Frank Spotnitz
Directed by: Frank Spotnitz
Summary: While Scully returns to teaching, Doggett and Reyes head to West Virginia to solve two ritualistic murders. A doctor at a mental hospital thinks one of the patients and a guard might have committed the murders. Another patient in the neighboring hospital room named Kobold claims he can hear the escaped patient and tells Doggett and Reyes that he has already killed again. The agents learn that Kobold was the mind behind the murders and that he chose his victims by their names.

Church
Wilshire United Methodist Church
711 S. Plymouth Blvd.
Los Angeles, Ca

Institution
The Ebell of Los Angeles
743 S. Lucerne Blvd.
Los Angeles, Ca

FBI Lecture Hall
Kinsey Hall
UCLA
Westwood Blvd.
Los Angeles, Ca

"I remember Frank was talking about the movie *Eyes Wide Shut* and there was this solo piano score, where one note kept repeating itself louder and faster," says Mark Snow when I asked him about the musical selection for *Daemonicus*. "He said he really liked that, and I did too, and there might be some places where that may work. There were a lot of solo instruments in that; it was great. I thought this show was very interesting and very well thought out; one of the best things Frank had ever done. It was a really great story and a wonderfully constructed script."

"I was one of the FBI cadets at UCLA in the classroom where she is teaching towards the entrance where Reyes and Doggett come in," fan LizzyX shares with me. "I was so stocked that Gillian Anderson was standing right there. I couldn't really hear them from where I was in the upper section, but they seemed to have a really good rapport and I could hear Gillian laughing."

<u>9x5 4-D</u>

Written by: Steven Maeda
Directed by: Tony Wharmby
Summary: Doggett is shot in an alley by a man named Lukesh while simultaneously at the apartment of Monica Reyes. When Doggett regains consciousness in the hospital, he tells Reyes she was with him on a stakeout and was severely injured. Reyes tells him she thinks he followed Lukesh through to a parallel universe and that when he came here he pushed her Doggett out. Doggett theorizes if Reyes pulls the plug he will go back to his universe and her Doggett will come back.

Erwin Timothy Lukesh Apartment
1305 W. Ingraham St.
Los Angeles, Ca

    This location is not in the best part of town. We had to wait in the car while a group of men stopped talking and went inside before I ventured out to photograph the site. Suffice to say, I did not stick around long enough for them to come back out.

9x06 Lord of the Flies

Written by: Thomas Schnauz
Directed by: Kim Manners
Summary: High School student Dylan Lokenguard secretes fly pheromones and can direct the behavior of flies. He directs them to kill one of his classmates and injure another. After attacking Agent Reyes and entomologist Dr. Bronzino, the boy and his mother disappear.

Garfield High School
Grant High School
13000 Oxnard St.
Sherman Oaks, Ca

Cheviot Hills Park
Dumbass Show Opening
2551 Motor Ave.
Los Angeles, Ca
***This site was also used for *The Unnatural* and *Three Words*

    "I played a high school student in this episode," recalls Adrienne Doucette. "I was happy to see Annabeth Gish on set at the high school, as I had never seen her in person before. I had previously seen Robert Patrick on the set of *Per Manum*. He was blasting Filter, his brother's band, which was awesome."

"I remember Kim being pretty cool towards us, because he thought we looked really young, which of course we were," shares LizzyX. "It's hard to remember, because when I was on the set, it's almost like I was in awe of everything since it was always my dream to be on *The X-Files* in some way, shape, or form and just being on the set. I was going to be part of television history for this amazing show. That feeling never wore off since I was getting to see these people in action and do what they do best."

9x08 Hellbound

Written by: David Amann
Directed by: Kim Manners
Summary: Men in an anger management group for criminals are having visions of men being skinned alive, before they are found skinned. Scully finds a similarity between these cases and a series of them from 1960. Scully exhumes two bodies from 1960s and finds the same weapon was used and that the death dates of the past victims are the birth dates of the current victims. Reyes believes that the men's souls are destined to be murdered time and again due to a crime that was committed, but never solved many years ago.

First Calvary Church
Church of the Angels
1100 Ave 64
Pasadena, Ca

Author's Note: This site was one of the more beautiful locations used in the show. While I am not a religious person, the architecture and the historical significance of this church was very moving and very much appreciated. Plus it was used in *The X-Files*, so extra cool bonus points.

9x14 Improbable

Written by: Chris Carter
Directed by: Chris Carter
Summary: Reyes shows Scully that three murders are connected by numerology. Scully and Reyes follow the killer into a parking garage and are trapped inside it with him. They meet "God" in the garage, and with nothing better to do, play checkers with him. During the game, Reyes has a realization about the case, the killer murders in threes; one blonde, one brunette, and one redhead. Doggett also discovers this pattern and ends the killing spree.

Normandie Casino
1045 W. Rosencrans Ave.
Gardena, Ca

9x15 Jump the Shark

Written by: Vince Gilligan, John Shiban, & Frank Spotnitz
Directed by: Cliff Bole
Summary: Ex Man-In-Black Morris Fletcher calls Doggett and Reyes for help but they don't believe anything he says until he mentions super soldiers. Doggett and Reyes go to the Lone Gunmen for help tracking down Eve Odell Harlow, Fletcher's supposed super soldier. When they find Eve, she tells them about a man carrying a deadly virus within himself. When the Gunmen catch the man, they are trapped in an air tight room with him, where the Gunmen are killed.

Los Angeles National Cemetery
950 S. Sepulveda Blvd.
Los Angeles, Ca

Conference Hotel
Marriot Hotel
333 S. Figueroa St.
Los Angeles, Ca

The return of Morris Fletcher to *The X-Files* made for an interesting episode. While the end of the show made many fans upset, the opening sequence at sea was visually spectacular. "We shot that boat blow up sequence on the back lot of Universal Studios," shares Harry Bring. "They have a huge cyclorama with a huge basin in front of it; all you see is sky. We filled the basin with water, launched the boats, and the rest is history. Blowing up something like that is real tedious and full of safety precautions. It took a whole day, with some of the scene shot first. It was life-sized and art department made that shell for the blow up boat look just like the real boat."

Editor's Note: you can see the cyclorama that Harry mentions on the studio backlot tour at Universal Studios. Check for hours and admission prices.

The view of the explosion from the Production boat. Photo by Harry Bring.

9x17 William

Written by: Chris Carter, Frank Spotnitz, & David Duchovny
Directed by: David Duchovny
Summary: Doggett is attacked in the office by a horribly disfigured man he thinks might be Mulder. The DNA tests point to Mulder, but Scully refuses to believe it is him. He tells Scully that William is part alien. The man, identified as Jeffrey Spender, goes into the nursery and injects William with magnetite. Scully fears for William's safety and is given up for adoption.

Van de Kamp Residence
Thornton Ranch
Ventura Farms
235 W. Potrero Ave.
Thousand Oaks, Ca

"I was on the FOX lot with a friend while they were filming *William* and prepping *Sunshine Days*," shares Kathleen Keegan. "We were walking around the set after lunch and we ran into Robert. Actually he almost ran into us. He was driving around the set in his pick-up truck and he saw us in street so he pretended like he was going to run us over. We began talking since he remembered us from previous shoots, and he told us about the Brady Bunch set up in one of the stages. We were allowed to go inside and see the set which was really cool."

9x16 Release

Written by: John Shiban & David Amann
Directed by: Kim Manners
Summary: Doggett follows a tip that leads to a connection between the murders of two women and his son, Luke. FBI cadet Hayes, a schizophrenic, believes victims of unsolved murders can speak to him. Doggett learns that Bob Harvey kidnapped his son, but he was killed by Harvey's boss after his son saw his face. Harvey's boss is shot by A.D. Follmer before Doggett can avenge Luke's death.

Cadet Rudolph Hayes Apartment
680 Witmer St.
Los Angeles, Ca

Mark Mooney's Bar
Boardner's
1652 N. Cherokee Ave.
Los Angeles, Ca

9x19 The Truth I & II

Written by: Chris Carter
Directed by: Kim Manners
Summary: Mulder is put on trial for the murder of super solider Knowle Rohrer. During the trial, Mulder refuses to testify and Scully, Jeffrey Spender, Marita Covarrubias, and Gibson Praise, are questioned about the X-Files, what they know about the existence of extraterrestrials, and the conspiracy to keep it silent. Mulder is found guilty and sentenced to death by lethal injection. Skinner and Kersh break Mulder out of the jail and he and Scully go to New Mexico where they meet the Cigarette-Smoking Man. He tells Scully what Mulder was reluctant to share with her, the truth about the alien invasion.

Fort MacArthur Military Base
Marine Mammal Care Center
(Leavenworth Dr./Osgood Farley Rd.)
3601 S. Gaffey St.
San Pedro, Ca

Anza-Borrego State Park
Borrego Springs, Ca

Snuggle Motel
La Cresenta Motel
2413 Foothill Blvd.
Glendale, Ca
***This site was also used in *Sein Und Zein* and *This Is Not Happening*

"In Borrego Springs on the series finale I went down early to prep for a couple of weeks," says Mac Gordon. "It was in the summer and it was mind bogglingly hot. Part of my job was to deal with the rangers on whose property we were operating in. I had to hire and walk through with the training crew with some biologists so that we could find the spiny back horned toad or something, so if we say it saw one or it was anywhere near our crew or activity, we could safely shuffle them off to some other part of the desert because they were endangered. Mind you, we were on a state park property that was an off road park, with motorcycles and ATV's flying all over the place, but they still blanched when I said we have to build Indian ruins and then blow it up.

The finished man made Indian ruins. Photo courtesy of Harry Bring.

That was the craziest thing I ever saw anyone do on any show I had worked on. It took some massaging, both locally and up in Sacramento to get it approved. It was great on television, but it was remarkable in person. There was also a crew game, that the actors would get involved in as well, but I can't remember the name. It involved passing around a ball, which you held for a certain amount of time and then you had to find the next person to pass them the ball. I don't remember the point of the game, but it was fun, but you defiantly wanted to be left holding the ball."

Don't Stop Believing

The writing of this book has been an adventure. While these past eighteen months have kept me pretty busy, I am elated that I am finally able to share the memories and stories from the Los Angeles cast and crew of *The X-Files* with fans all over the world. I hope this book can serve as inspiration to lead your own expedition.

Acknowledgements

I would like to say a special thank the following people for helping to make this book a reality and a success.

To Joy Krone, Adrienne Doucette, Mac Gordon, and Kathleen Keegan for providing me with the location information in this book.

To all the cast and crew of *The X-Files*. Thank you for your memories.

To my great friends: Courtney Smith, Karen Mendez, and Dayna Loder. Thank you for keeping me on track during those long hours and helping me structure the book. And then restructure again.

To Angie Cotrell: for guiding me through the prep process. Your "thinking outside of the box" in areas was a godsend.

To Mya Brown and Patricia Steffy: without your help, I would not have been able to track down various cast and crew.

An extra special thanks to Jana Fain: when I hit a wall, you knocked it down and allowed me to continue my journey.

To Melanie Muller: for putting her creative powers to use and designing the beautiful artwork. You rock Sis!

To B. Sandu Anelice and F.C. Mansour: for their breathtaking video compilations.

To Karla Paes: Thank you for all your hard work.

And finally, to Mrs. Money Penny: thank you for putting up with those long, numerous hours in the car.

I would also like to extend my gratitude to:

Allair, Matt	Devol, Tiffany
Amrein, Carmen	Duchovny, David
Anderson, Gillian	Frieberg, Connie
Apolina92	Gilligan, Vince
Beck, Mat	Gish, Annabeth
Big Light Network	Goodwin, R.W.
Bobilya, Cassie	Gordon, Howard
Borden, Amy	Gordon, Mac
Bowman, Rob	Gulka, Jeff
Braidwood, Tom	Haglund, Dean
Bring, Harry	Harwood, Bruce
Cantrell, Julie	Holden, Laurie
Carolvee	Hurwitz, Matt
Childers, Michael	Hutchinson, Genny
Davis, William	Jack, Nina

Jackson, Guy	Robinson, Tiffany
Jones, Ilt	Roe, Bill
Joy, Charissa	Rotter, Gabe
Kajikami, Mindy	Sackheim, Dan
Larken, Sheila	Schnauz, Tom
LizzyX	Shull, Janet
Lopez, Jacqueline	Snow, Mark
MacDougal, Heather	Spotnitz, Frank
MacLaren, Michelle	Stemme, Marlene
Mayers, Corren	Strand, Jill-Hege
Morgan, Glen	Studor, Eleanore
Orodromenus	The X-Files Lexicon
Paes, Karla	Thomas, Barry
Patrick, Robert	Thompson, Brian
Philiater	Vera, Julia
Pileggi, Mitch	Watkins, Michael
Quijada, Avi	X Files News
Rabwin, Paul	

Made in the USA
Charleston, SC
08 December 2010